Prepper Community

A Group-Based Methodology for Planning and Operating a Survival Retreat

Copyright © 2018 Thomas Eddy

All rights reserved.

No part of this publication may be reproduced, distributed, or transmitted in any form or by any means, including photocopying, recording, or other electronic or mechanical methods, without the prior written permission of the author, except in the case of brief quotations embodied in critical reviews and certain other noncommercial uses permitted by copyright law.

For permission requests, contact the author at ThomasEddyPrepping@gmail.com.

Written by Thomas Eddy.
Illustrations and cover design by Earl Koenig.

First Printing: 2018

ISBN-13: 978-1978487758

Disclaimer: This book is intended to be used for educational and reference purposes only. While every effort was made to ensure the quality and accuracy of the information contained herein, the author and publisher are not responsible or liable for any alleged injury or damages resulting directly or indirectly from its use.

Preface

The unprepared are a predictable bunch, and most people fall into this category. What starts with civil unrest and rioting will end with panic and starvation. Some folks' "best case scenario" will involve refugee camps and food lines. For most, the reality will be much grimmer. When the populated urban centers have become cesspools of death, disease, and human waste, the only salvation for those stranded within will be for death to come swiftly.

For those who are prepared and are truly dedicated to surviving, their outlook is much brighter. Life is about priorities and choices. For most, social media and reality television are among the top day-to-day priorities. For the average

Thomas Eddy

American, going out of town on vacation or saving up for a larger television are "long-term objectives". For a very tenacious few, getting prepared for the "what if" that is looming over our society's head is a continuous priority, and having a plan in place to continue living should the worst happen is the ultimate long-term objective.

The Blackout of 2003

When one single part of our system goes down for even a couple days, we observe a frightening indication of how bad things could quickly become if some or all parts of our system were to shut down indefinitely. In 2003, the Northeastern United States and parts of Canada experienced a large-scale failure of the power grid. Among the many states and provinces which were affected by this power grid failure were several densely-populated cities including New York City, NY, Cleveland, OH, Detroit, MI, and Toronto, ON (just to name a few). In all, an estimated 55 million people were without power for between one and three days.

The frightening effects of this power failure started immediately. Traffic signals didn't work, so there was gridlock on every street and highway. The few gas stations with backup generators which were able to remain open had lines of cars a mile long waiting to fill up their tanks (which also led to incredible price gouging and sky-high tension between citizens). So the majority of people could not purchase gasoline for transportation or for their personal generators. Oil refineries were forced to shut down temporarily, which exacerbated the disruption of gasoline supplies that were experienced in the coming weeks.

No restaurants were open. No grocery stores were open. I located one crusty convenience store near my home which was still selling items for cash. I stocked up on a few bags of chips and candy bars, as it was pretty much the only food they had.

Cities which rely heavily on public transit were even more affected. Commuters were trapped in stalled subway cars. Passenger trains were not operating.

Airports essentially shut down because of the electrical equipment needed for just about every aspect of operation.

Mobile phone communication was crippled, due to power loss at cellular sites. People were unable to get in touch with family and friends to find out if they were safe. The loss of electrical power led to a multi-faceted breakdown of most modern conveniences and municipal services.

During the first day, spirits were not particularly low in my neighborhood. For the people who were not stuck somewhere in unrelenting traffic, there was almost a festive atmosphere. As it was summer, folks were grilling up all of the meat in their fridges before it went bad. People up and down the neighborhoods were holding impromptu block parties and barbecues. However, by the second day the mood began to quickly change. There was no more unspoiled meat to grill up. Most areas still had water service to some degree, though it was advised that tap water be boiled before consuming.

There were no street lights. The demand for police assistance around the cities was far too great for local law enforcement agencies to keep up on. By the beginning of night #2, groups of people were roaming the streets. I'm not sure if they were simply bored, or if they were looking to improve their situation by worsening the situation of others. I chose not to approach them to ask. Rioting and looting was reported in some areas. People felt helpless, and fear and desperation were already beginning to creep in. It had only been two days since this one common utility went down. One single cog in our modern clockwork of infrastructure, and it was only two days before society in several large metropolitan areas came dreadfully close to unraveling. This was the experience which first opened my eyes to the frailty of our system on which most of our very lives depend.

What Are We Preparing for?

If you are reading this, then chances are strong that you've previously considered the possibility that life as we know it could abruptly change due to some circumstance outside of our control. There are millions of people in the United States who identify as "preppers" or "survivalists." The reasons behind why these people feel it necessary to diligently prepare are a vast array of theories and speculation. Many citizens worry that our fragile power grid or other utilities will fail on a grand scale, causing the food supply and every other piece of infrastructure to subsequently grind to a halt. Some believe that a nuclear war will erupt between The United States and another world superpower. Others believe climate change will spur a series of cataclysmic natural disasters. Many of those concerned for the future of civilization abide by the notion that inevitable global financial collapse will lead to our currency being worthless, ultimately sparking civil unrest and spiraling out of control into a complete societal meltdown. A fair number of preppers are afraid that a new civil war will break out between the United States government and its citizens.

Regardless of which global, national, or regional incident leads to the breakdown of our modern way of life, the outcome is bound to be, more or less, the same. When people can't afford or otherwise can't access the resources they need, panic and desperation ensue. When panic and desperation ensue, violence is sure to follow. If everybody worked together for the greater good, the outcome would *still* be questionable because of how many people will be in need of resources. But people don't tend to work together in times of prolonged crisis. Those who respect life the least are bound to take advantage of those who are weaker, both mentally and physically. People will kill and steal over a can of food or a drink of water. Others will kill simply because there are no legal consequences. Mothers, fathers, sons, and daughters will become killers – either in defending against evil people or because they, themselves are desperate for resources.

Looting, vandalism, death, destruction, and rape will be commonplace. And it will not take very long after the system crashes for this reality to foment. In August of 2005, Hurricane Katrina caused unimaginable destruction to Louisiana and Mississippi. Much of New Orleans was under water, millions of people were without electricity, and help was slow to arrive. Some people were stranded in (or on) their homes for a long time. Within a day after the hurricane moved on from New Orleans, the violence and crime began. Incidents of looting, robbery, car-jacking, murder, and rape were rampant. While some claimed that they took only food from stores, the rest of the country watched on the evening news as looters trudged through floodwaters, holding freshly-plundered flat-screen televisions over their heads.

Those who weren't doomed to remain trapped within the flooded wreckage were taken to refugee camps. Hundreds of thousands of people who evacuated their homes were kept in makeshift facilities around neighboring states. The Red Cross and National Guard brought in what supplies they could. This was life for the lucky. Food and water lines, sleeping on cots or the floor, and waiting in line to use a toilet were the luxuries they enjoyed. Packed together like a crawling pile of humanity, these were the "lucky ones" who relied on being saved by the government during a time of crisis.

This was one localized region in the United States. Every other part of the country was perfectly intact and capable of sending aid and supplies to the affected region. Legions of law enforcement personnel, construction workers, and all manner of aid workers flocked to Louisiana and Mississippi in the aftermath of Hurricane Katrina to help with the recovery efforts. But what if every region in the United States is in trouble? What if there are too many people for the government to rescue? What if the "rescue" is more horrible than what you're being rescued from?

The vast majority of Americans rely on the efforts of thousands of machines, computers, and other people just to live their day-to-day lives. From our utilities, to access to our money, to getting something to eat for lunch, we are at the mercy of a massively intricate and interwoven web of services and infrastructure. It's unsettling and inconvenient to think about, but every one of the systems and processes that make up this delicate web of modern life are startlingly fragile and vulnerable. It would take less than most people like to believe for everything to spiral out of control. All it takes is for a couple of services to stop working on a large scale, and before you know it there will be pandemonium.

And those who are responsible for our services and supply chains, even parts that aren't necessarily initially affected, are just regular people. They will become part of the dissolution, just like everybody else. When fear takes hold, the guy who is scheduled to deliver a truck full of groceries to your supermarket will not be a truck driver on that day. He will be a husband, father, son, or simply a scared individual. When panic ensues, the people in charge of keeping your mobile phone service and internet up and running will no longer be technicians who give a damn about your service. They will be mothers, sisters, brothers, uncles, or simply frantic human beings. These folks will be concerned about themselves and their families – not you and yours. Your need for groceries and internet can go to hell. What do you do for a living? Will you go to work the day that half of America loses electricity? If the grocery store shelves are baron and panic is spreading through the streets, will you be heading into the office to catch up on your spreadsheets? The point I'm trying to thoroughly drive home is that our modern way of life is supported by a house of cards that has been built in tornado alley.

This is why we prep. If "the shit hits the fan," no matter what that means to you, are you willing to risk the safety and lives of yourself and your family to a government agency that may or may not even be able to help? Are you going to sit around and fall victim to the desperation, violence, and destruction happening all around you? If you are reading this, then chances are probably strong that you already consider it preferable to be in charge of your own fate, should the shit hit the proverbial fan.

What if it's Only Temporary?

Throughout our nation's history, every disaster that has led to widespread panic, hunger, homelessness, and absence of civil services has been a temporary situation. The United States has experienced disasters which caused people's lives to be disrupted for days, weeks, or months. But in each case, people end up tightening their belts, pulling up their bootstraps, and getting the problem sorted out. Short of a full-scale catastrophe or chain reaction of infrastructure failures, most disaster scenarios are not likely to indefinitely change the face of this country as we know it. So far, this country has survived and rebuilt after plenty of natural disasters, utility service failures, and civil unrest.

If something disrupts the supply chain, infrastructure, or societal foundation and is likely to be a temporary circumstance, then sheltering in place is a viable course of action. If you have prepped all you will need for several months, and your place of shelter can physically withstand the circumstances, it is entirely possible that you can outlast an incident which is ultimately fixable.

For example, if the power grid goes down in your area for several months but it's being actively repaired, you can survive. If there was a natural disaster that disrupted the food supply to your town, but your home is unscathed, you can hunker down and ride it out. Your biggest concern will be security at that point, because most people who will be affected even temporarily will soon become desperate. Think about how much food is in your pantry right now. Most households in the United States don't have more than a few days' worth of food at any given time. It won't be too long before most families have depleted even the last old can of lima beans from their cupboard. FEMA and Red Cross water trucks, food lines, and the National Guard will become the way of life for most people in the area until everything is restored to normal. Just looking at photos of displaced people and refugees after Hurricane Katrina is enough to make me want to be able to take care of myself in the aftermath of something like that. If you have stored food, water, supplies, and security measures in your home, and your home is still a viable place to remain after an event that causes a disruption in services, you will be in a much better position than most. This is where your stores of dried foods, water, and supplies come in. As long as you can keep others from taking what you have, you can ride it out and wait until order and services are restored. Canned food, water barrels, and firewood will keep you going nicely -- but only until they run out. I believe most people who engage in "prepping" are equipped to survive a scenario of completely independent living for no more than a few months.

However, if your entire state or country is undergoing a scenario in which you will likely be without the supply chain or social order, it's going to be very serious. The United States is resilient. It craves order and normalcy. No matter how big of a disaster, we've always bounced back. Most disasters are somewhat localized. Hurricanes, earthquakes, tornadoes, terrorist attacks, and rioting are events that occur in relatively isolated locations (in the grand scheme of things). The recovery and rebuilding initiatives happen quickly and with a lot of resources. Federal aid, state aid, and the assistance from surrounding cities and even other countries make for a somewhat speedy recovery of services. We will clean, repair, rebuild, and resupply everything in an impressive amount of time, as long as we are able to do so.

But imagine an event or scenario where this was unable to happen. Such an event would have to be so big or far-reaching that the entire country, region, or world is also affected. If everybody needs help, there is nobody available to help. If this is the case, and an incident or chain of events took place that brought down the entire country's social structure and supply chain, then what we're really talking about at this point is a total collapse of society. If this happens, nothing in our lifetimes will likely ever be the same. If it does go back to anything resembling "normal", it's going to take a very long time. Police officers, soldiers, medical professionals, sanitation workers, farmers, and everybody in between who are responsible for keeping our civilization running will no longer be people of those professions. They will be fathers, mothers, husbands, wives, brothers, and sisters who are now worried about the very survival of their families and themselves.

What I'm getting at is if a disaster or event takes place which is sure to be temporary, then sheltering in place at your home is plausible. But if something takes place that is bound to leave society broken down for greater than several months, then it's a safe bet that society will be broken down for a lot *longer* than several months. And if you are left on your own in a true WROL/SHTF scenario for an indefinite amount of time, it's a very bad idea to stay anywhere near a heavily populated urban or suburban environment.

To recap: For a short-term survival situation where rule of law, the supply chain, and infrastructure will almost certainly be restored in the foreseeable future, you may be fine to shelter in place at your home if you are equipped and capable of doing so. But if we're talking about a long-term survival situation where the very fabric of our civilization has crumbled, you'd better get as far away from the hordes of starving, thirsty, lawless, unprepared people as you can. How do you prepare for this sort of situation? How will you survive and thrive after getting the hell out of town? That's what this book is all about.

There are a lot of publications about emergency preparedness, homesteading, food storage/preservation, and everything in between. What this book aims to present is a road map for how to go about planning and establishing a "survival community," which I believe provides the best chances and outlook for surviving the long-term after a collapse of what we currently recognize as society.

Contents

1. Survival Community Overview.................................. 15
2. Organizing with Others.. 25
3. Establishing an Operational Plan.......................... 37
4. Choosing an Ideal Location for Your Retreat........ 51
5. Building and Prepping Your Retreat...................... 67
6. Bugging Out.. 87
7. Retreat Activation.. 95
8. Leadership and Member Roles............................. 99
9. Food.. 103
10. Water... 107
11. Heat... 113
12. Power... 117
13. Sanitation... 121
14. Security.. 125
15. New Members After SHTF................................... 131
16. Disaster Prevention and Recovery....................... 135
17. Morale.. 139
18. Recommended Resources................................... 143

Chapter 1
Survival Community Overview

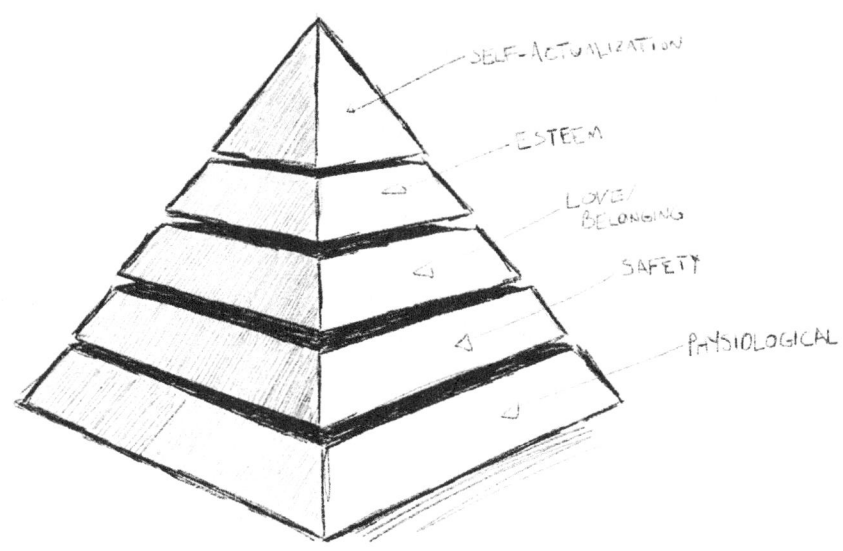

It's not impossible to stay alive by yourself, with no other human resources to help you. It can be done. It has been done. People have survived, alone, in the middle of the wilderness since the dawn of mankind. That was once the way of the world. People were raised to develop the knowledge and skills needed to live off the land. However, for a developed and modern place like present-day America, almost none of us have the skills, knowledge, physical capabilities, or frame of mind to suddenly begin fending 100% for ourselves. Most of us can't do it, and most of us wouldn't want to do it. We're accustomed to our way of life full of structure and modern conveniences. We eat food that other people harvested, in homes that other people built. We drive to work in a car that took thousands of people to create and we plug away at our job where we are a tiny part of a larger operation. Sure, we still have blacksmiths and lumberjacks and true tradesmen. But the majority of Americans make a living from being a cog in the machine. Many Americans make a living doing a job that will have very little practical use if civilized society collapses. The point I'm aiming to make is that we live in a society that has been built to rely on infrastructure, mass production, consumerism, and complacency. This is the nature of modern society as we've created it.

So what happens when the SHTF and our entire modern system of living no longer functions? We know the answer to that, and that is why we prep. But prepping alone isn't going to make everything OK. While many preppers are incredibly dedicated and are going to fantastic lengths to secure their futures and their families' futures should the worst happen, it's not enough. Storing enough food and supplies for you and your family to live off of for ten years is amazing, but it's not enough. Assuming you can keep looters and cut-throats away from your family and your supplies, you could survive. Assuming a natural disaster doesn't destroy everything you've worked so hard to store, staying alive for years to come is a definite possibility. But "staying not dead" and "living" are two entirely different things.

I'll use the prison analogy here: The most dangerous, horrible prisoners in a maximum security penitentiary can live in solitary confinement for decades. They are kept alive with food, water, and the most basic of physiological needs. From a security standpoint, they are also arguably the "safest" of any prisoner. But that is not "living," according to any interpretation of the word that I believe in. Even the "general population" prisoners are able to have human interaction - even relationships. They can socialize, they can partake in recreational activities. Some of them are able to work and be productive and/or creative. The people who are in solitary confinement are deprived of any physical or psychological stimulation. They are experiencing the technical processes of having a living body, and that's about it. Is this how your family wants to live out their days? Holed-up in a bunker, eating your five-thousandth freeze-dried meal from a sealed pouch?

I like the prison analogy, because it gives a rough idea of the concept I regularly preach. It's not a perfect analogy, because I don't necessarily like the idea of equating "survival" with "being in a prison". Nevertheless, I consider it of utmost importance that if humanity must resort to a "survivalist" lifestyle as a result of a large-scale breakdown of modern society, our objective should not be to simply "survive." Our objective should be to survive *and* thrive.

Hierarchy of Needs

In the 1940s, renowned psychologist Abraham Maslow published a paper that outlines what has come to be known as "Maslow's Hierarchy of Needs". For those who are not familiar with Maslow's Hierarchy of Needs, I will explain. Maslow broke down and categorized everything that a human feels the "need" for in his or her lifetime. The Hierarchy is often presented as a pyramid-shaped chart. The idea is that the lowest (and thus widest) levels of the pyramid are the most basic needs. The most basic needs must be fulfilled before a person would consider the next level of the pyramid to truly be something that he or she needs.

Physiological
What do you need to physically stay alive? Every human needs oxygen, water, food, and protection from the elements (clothing, shelter, etc.).

Safety
Humans need to be safe and feel safe. This level can pertain to any part of the spectrum of feeling "safe," be it security from physical danger, financial security, or anything in between.

Love/Belonging
If a human's physiological and safety needs are fulfilled, a person will feel the

need to "belong." Generally speaking, unless people are starving or in constant physical danger, they long for the feelings of friendship, intimacy, family, and being loved.

Esteem

The next level of need that people feel is to be important. Who doesn't like the feeling of being recognized for something at work or in a social circle? The need for esteem may include longing for status, fame, or attention. It may also materialize as a need for self-improvement (esteem for oneself).

Self-Actualization

I think it can be argued that many pursue this need, but almost no one truly fulfills it. The highest level in the Hierarchy of Needs is to accomplish everything that one possibly *could* accomplish. To do so would mean that, on your death bed, you could say to yourself, "I've done everything I could ever do, and I've become everything I could possibly become."

Why do I bring up the Hierarchy of Needs? Let's go back to the prison analogy. The solitary confinement prisoner has the two most basic levels of needs fulfilled (physiological and safety). But that's it. That is living, but only according to the strict dictionary definition of the word.

Let's talk about it from a point of view that is more practical to a scenario where people must live after SHTF. You can live in your bunker with your family, and eat your stored rice and canned meat. As long as you stay invisible and constantly alert, you can stay alive. This will be your life: Huddled in a safe-room, eating freeze-dried meals, sitting for potentially years on end in a state of constant fear and monotony.

This is how it will be if you intend to have your physiological and safety needs fulfilled with only yourself or a couple other people to rely on. The majority of preppers who I know are not planning to hide out in a bunker for years on end. They plan to grow gardens, filter rainwater, and possibly raise animals for meat. But if it's only them and their small families to manage an operation like that, there are simply too many "wildcard" factors and loose ends that can lead to failure (and we all know what "failure of a survival plan" means). As humans, we want to have a life where we can pursue the fulfillment of all our needs. In order to do this, the "hide in a bunker" method is simply no option. Living and thriving means working, playing, growing, and loving with other people. Hypothetically this can be accomplished within one average family unit of three to eight people. But in a practical sense, this does not equate to enough "manpower" to maintain what will need to be maintained in a self-sufficient survivalist environment. A community is the only way.

The "Joe" Example

Let me lay out an example scenario that I believe is considered somewhat "ideal" to a lot of dedicated preppers:

Something has caused a panic among the population. Civil society is beginning to unravel as a result of some event (collapse of financial system, catastrophic power grid failure, class wars; choose your poison). A man (let's call him Joe), his wife, and three children have bugged-out to their remote homestead. Since Joe has been a dedicated prepper for years, his family's survival retreat is well-equipped and well-supplied.

On the property is a log cabin, outfitted with solar power, a wood-burning stove, and rainwater collection system. An outhouse has been constructed out behind the home. There is also a large storage shed next to the cabin, which easily holds the food, supplies, and water that Joe has prepared. Joe has stockpiled nonperishable food, water, and all essential supplies. With the stockpile alone, Joe and his family should be able to last for a couple of years before running out of anything. He has established redundancy for the most essential supplies, such as water filtration and heating appliances.

The property is off the beaten path, a hundred miles from the nearest city, and consists of woodlands as well as a large, empty yard. The woods can provide for hunting, and the yard is perfect for an elaborate garden. Vegetable seeds, composting containers, and farming equipment have been accumulated and stored onsite. Joe even has a small coop full of chickens and a rooster, which can provide meat and eggs for years to come.

The homestead boasts an arsenal of weaponry for security and hunting purposes. Joe has a deer rifle, a couple of AR-15s, a 12-guage shotgun, a variety of pistols, and crates full of ammunition for each weapon. Joe's wife and oldest son also know how to use the firearms, and will play a role in security/defense measures if necessary.

Joe has supplies for medical emergencies, sanitation, and food prep. He has worked out processes for water filtration and food storage. Months' worth of firewood, propane, and gasoline have also been gathered and stored.

As someone who has been establishing my preparations for quite some time, this sounds like a pretty sweet setup. But as much time and money as Joe and his family have spent to procure supplies and stock their homestead with everything they need to live, there are a few major problems. All that hard work and money won't be enough.

Sure, somebody like Bill Gates could build a Mega-Compound with state-of-the-art technology powered by geothermal energy, laser-guided aerial guard drones, on-site water processing facility, and an autonomous factory that turns trespassers into Soylent Green. If I had billions of dollars to spend on my doomsday survival compound, there is no limit to what I could dream up. If money was no object, then I could build a mile-high wall around a ten-thousand acre compound, with sentry machine guns and an entirely self-reliant utopia operated and maintained by my army of robot servants. But of course that isn't realistic for me, and the probability is high that it's not realistic for you. Joe's setup is about as good as it gets for us regular folks.

So what are the problems that Joe faces with his survival retreat? He's got supplies, food, water, weapons, etc. What could go wrong? Why would Joe and his family be better off in a community of 20-30 people than by themselves?

First and foremost, security is going to be an enormous concern. One skilled man with a rifle and a painfully-empty stomach is all that stands between a promising future for Joe's family and absolutely no future. OK, I get that most people aren't military snipers. How about a small team of raiders wielding pistols or machetes? In a situation where electronic-oriented technology is useless and law enforcement officers don't exist, it would take only the element of surprise and/or a few determined individuals to completely overrun Joe's homestead. It could take only moments for Joe's survivalist utopia to become *their* survivalist utopia. It could take Joe and his family moments to go from sleeping peacefully to "resting in peace". It's a grim reality, but it's reality. As I've said, there are few lines people aren't willing to cross when they're on the verge of starvation or dehydration. Even if Joe saw the bad guys coming and was able to get into a full defensive shooting position with his wife and oldest son, they are at a severe disadvantage. They're pinned down. They are sitting ducks, and the bad guys know it. The best case scenario is killing the bad guys and not suffering any causalities. The best outcome of this attempted invasion is that the homestead is successfully defended... this time.

Security concerns are perhaps the most severe in such an environment, but they are certainly not the only ones. Gardening is a full time job for a family of five. Gathering, filtering, and storing water is another full time job to satisfy the hydration needs of five people. How about hunting or tending to livestock? How much firewood needs to get gathered and chopped to make it through the winter months? Food prep, sanitation, and general maintenance are constant necessities. I don't doubt that two determined adults, one teenager, and a couple of young children could take a noble stab at running a homestead in a situation like this. But there is so much left to chance. Even without constant security concerns, there is simply too much to be done by so few people.

The Two Principles

I've been attempting to answer the question, "Why would I need more people than my immediate family to successfully run a survival retreat?" Understanding the following two principles is key to realizing why operating as a community is so advantageous from a logistics standpoint.

Consolidation of Efforts

Several people can each do a smaller amount of work to achieve a goal that the entire group will benefit from.

Compounding of Efforts

Several people can accomplish proportionately more than fewer people (AKA: The whole is greater than the sum of its parts).

One person cannot do as much work, proportionately speaking, as several people. For example, try to move a couch from your basement to your living room all by yourself. I guarantee it will take more than twice the time and work than if you had a second person to help.

Two people can accomplish proportionately more than one person can. And twenty people can accomplish proportionately more than five people can. Instead of five families digging five separate latrines, everyone can pitch in and dig one latrine for all five families. Instead of five families building a fence around five properties, everybody can contribute and build one fence around one property. Do you see where I'm going with this? Instead of five individual families who are responsible for securing and patrolling five separate perimeters, five families together can be much more effective at patrolling one perimeter.

When it comes to surviving in an unforgiving world where the grid is down, technology and money are worthless, and the cavalry isn't coming, you owe it to yourself and your family to give yourselves the best possible chance

of success. Being part of a community that is working in consort towards a common objective is easier *and* more effective than going it alone.

Summary

A lot of preppers and survivalists don't fully subscribe to the "community-based" methodology for a survival compound. Many of our like-minded brethren have adopted an, "If you aren't me, you're my enemy." philosophy about the world post-SHTF. Plenty of folks have already made up their minds about how their survival operation should be run, and that is nobody's business but their own. For those of you who are on the fence about the whole concept, here are the key points I want you to consider:

- If you want to survive *and* thrive, holing up in a bunker for the rest of your life is not an option.
- If you want to live and grow with your family through homesteading, it's dangerous and incredibly difficult to do it alone.
- Being part of a larger survival community will provide social value (friendship, love, esteem, etc).
- Community efforts are consolidated and compounded, allowing for more people to achieve greater things while doing less work.

Chapter 2
Organizing with Others

With the ever-growing concern for what the future holds, combined with the increasing popularity of "prepper culture" in America, more people than ever are actively involved in planning and preparing for the worst. This means that the number of forward-thinking, like-minded folks are increasing by the day. That is the good news. However, the difficulty lies in the fact that we are scattered all throughout the country, and that we aren't particularly easy to identify. Not being easily identified is indeed one of the unwritten tenets of prepping, as it's simply common sense to keep your activities on a "need to know" basis with other people. It's probable that you know at least one other person who is actively involved in some level of prepping, without you even realizing it. How many of your neighbors are preppers? How many of your neighbors know that *you* are a prepper? I bet the answer is "Few to none."

Most publications on this topic estimate the current number of active preppers in the United States to be around 3 million. That's not a whole lot in the grand scheme of things. There are currently around 320,000,000 people living in the United States. That means less than 1% of the country's population is actively engaged in preparing for a SHTF scenario.

The community-based survival methodology revolves around forming a group with other like-minded people. Ideally, such a group should already be established and ready well in advance of a catastrophe. Trying to put together a group of desperate strangers *after* society begins to crumble is going to be exponentially more difficult and dangerous.

While probably more common in rural and remote areas of the country, lots of people are already related to or acquainted with other preppers. These are the people who already have the hardest part figured out. Even if they don't yet have quite enough people for an ideal survival community, they've already gotten off to a great start.

The exact number of people that should comprise your survival community will vary, depending on the size and geographical location of the property, proximity to densely-populated cities, resources available to you, and other factors. Generally speaking, a minimum of fifteen to twenty able-bodied people should be in your community. When you break it down, that's about four or five average-sized families coming together to establish a strong, productive, and safe retreat.

So how can a person who is motivated to organize a SHTF survival community go about finding other like-minded people with whom to band together? It's not quite as simple as trying to start a book club or organize a poker game. Those who don't understand why we do what we do are often quick to judge us as "nuts". In the name of self-preservation, it's not exactly advisable to send out a mass email to your entire office with a subject line of, "Hey, is anyone interested in running away to the woods with me after the apocalypse?" Organizing anything that is considered even slightly controversial requires a bit more thought.

There are two categories of people with whom you should start a dialog about the matter at hand: People who already know you, and people who are of the same mindset as you. People with whom you already have a relationship will know that you're not "nuts," and are more likely to hear you out. And like-minded people, such as other preppers and survivalists, don't consider such things to be "nuts" in the first place.

At the end of the day, your objective is to find other people whom you believe would be assets to a survival community. You don't want just any random person to get involved. You need committed people who will devote time and resources to the project. People with essential skill sets, experience, or resources will be your greatest assets.

So who should you talk to? Who should be on your short list of people to approach? How does a person break the ice on this subject? Here are some good places to start with identifying and approaching prospects.

Talk to other preppers whom you already know

This one is a no-brainer. If you already have a rapport or relationship with other people whom you know to already be involved in prepping, this is the first place to start. The biggest hurdle in forming a group of survival-conscious people is actually convincing them that survival prep is important. With other survivalists, they already know!

Not only will other preppers already be on the same page as you, they are likely to have already been establishing their own preps, formulating their own plan, and developing their own skills. All you really need to do is persuade them that the benefits of collaborating are too great to dismiss (remember *Consolidation of Efforts* and *Compounding of Efforts*).

As always, keep in mind that you should choose people based on how much of an asset they will be. This can mean many things. If your best friend has no specialized skills or resources, he may still an "asset" because he is your best friend. Companionship and friendship have value, and thus are an asset. Though what I really want to highlight with regards to choosing people is more about who *not* to choose. You want assets; not liabilities. Anybody who is not likely to be a liability can probably be considered an asset, assuming he/she is an able-bodied person who is dedicated to the cause. What you don't want is somebody who is going to cause problems or be altogether useless.

For example, let's say you are acquainted with a guy who is a die-hard prepper, has lots of resources, is an experienced outdoorsman, but happens to be a huge jerk who can't get along with anybody. This is not a guy you want on your team. Everything will turn into a problem. Everything will become a fight. This is the last thing you want. In a survival community, everybody has to be on the same page. When disagreements arise, they must be resolved with reason and civility. Bull-headed jerks, shifty criminals, and angry drunks are a few examples of the sort of folks you should not consider for your survival community. The list could go on and on, but my point is that you should be very selective in who you approach to be part of your community.

Encourage close friends and family members to consider the benefits of being prepared

If you're a prepper, chances are good that a few people in your family or circle of friends are aware of it, to at least some degree. Perhaps your friends and loved ones are familiar with the general idea of what you've been up to, or otherwise get the gist of what it means to prep. Either way, anybody who already knows (and likes) you, even if you are the "paranoid survival guy," are all potential members to enlist.

So some degree or other, many of my friends and extended family members are aware of my dedication to preparedness. Some of them think it's silly. Some of them find it fascinating. Some of them think I'm downright mentally ill. But almost every one of them says things like, "Well I know where *I'm* going if the apocalypse actually happens!" Even if presented in a sort of joking manner, it's obvious that they truly would have few other options than to try and seek my help. Regardless of how unlikely they believe a SHTF scenario is to occur, it seems that they all keep it in the back of their minds that horning in on *my* years of hard work, expense, and knowledge would be a wholly tangible option (if not their only option).

Obviously, having every family member and friend you know suddenly showing up to your place after the grid goes down is not going to work in most cases. I'd love to take care of everybody I know with only the resources I personally have, but it's not possible. Again, Bill Gates could do it. He can have a fully-functioning doomsday community, just ready for ten thousand survivors to occupy it at a moment's notice. My point is that it's not necessarily a great thing that your friends and family think of you as their plan. "Why bother doing all that work and spending all that money when 'ol Bob over there is already doing all that? I'll just grab my sleeping bag and head over to his place if everything goes to hell." I won't bother going into detail about the grim reality that those folks would face if they all tried to show up at Bob's place and expect to be taken care of. This isn't the reason I bring all of this up. The reason for discussing it is to point out that many of those who have shown no interest in prepping for themselves have still acknowledged, to *some* degree, that such a thing could be necessary. Why would they even think to make the joke about going to 'ol Bob's place if they were absolutely certain and convinced that such preparations would never serve a purpose?

Unless you're a millionaire, you probably can't establish the sort of setup that would be required to provide refuge for everybody you know. That's the reality. But what you can do is talk to the people you already know and urge them to consider helping themselves. The more people who are prepping, the fewer people you need to worry about helping (or not being able to help). And when it comes to a community-based survival methodology, more preppers means more potential assets to be part of the group.

When initiating a serious discussion with a non-prepper about the benefits of prepping, it's not wise to start right off with the doomsday theories like global pandemic or full scale attacks on the United States. These ideas are so far-fetched to most people that it's going to only deepen their preconceived notion that preppers are some kind of "nuts". People who have not fully realized the fragility of our modern way of life need to be eased into it. Describe something much more relatable to the average person when breaking the ice about prepping. What are things that would affect everybody immediately? What things are far more likely to happen, because they already do? Power outages are somewhat common in most parts of the country, and with our modern way of living it immediately presents a massive inconvenience to most people. No TV, computer, video game, coffee maker, hair dryer, etc. Even a very short power outage can ruin your whole day. It doesn't take a lot to get somebody to think about how unpleasant it would be to completely lose power for a whole week. How about a month?

I like to tell people about the experience which first got me thinking about preparing for disaster. The Northeast blackout of 2003 only lasted a couple of days, and most people came out of it basically unscathed. But as you and I know, things could have gotten very ugly very fast if that outage lasted just a couple *more* days. I describe to people how I only had about three day's worth of food in my house (and that would have been seriously scraping the bottom of the barrel). The grid doesn't care if it's been awhile since you went grocery shopping. The grid doesn't care if you planned on filling up your gas tank tomorrow. When it's down, it's down, and you'd better already have on hand what you need to get through it.

Most people can understand the blackout example. Heck, most of the people I know experienced it personally. But most people don't ever really think about what would happen if a blackout lasted for weeks or months. The best-case scenario for most people would be Red Cross food and water lines. People would be displaced, possibly crammed into a sports arena that was turned into a makeshift refugee camp. If a blackout occurred for just a few weeks on a regional or national scale, it would affect every aspect of our lives, possibly for months or years to come.

"What if you had the capability to be entirely self-reliant for between six months and a year?"

It's not difficult to explain to somebody how much better their life would be during those six months than the lives of all those people who must rely 100% on help from others to simply stay alive. Presenting the whole concept of prepping as a solution for a shorter-term (and thus more realistic and relatable) problem makes the whole thing seem not only more reasonable to a skeptical person, but more palatable. When something seems too far-fetched or difficult, so many people just withdraw completely, often to the point of denial.

"It's too difficult to lose weight and get into shape, so why bother even trying? Renovating the kitchen is so much work, so let's just live with the rotted cabinets and rusty old sink. Why even worry about living if the system goes down since it would be so impossible to even prepare for such a thing?"

If you can change their idea that prepping automatically means storing grain in a bunker to last for a hundred years, people begin to get more open-minded. FEMA advises all Americans to keep three days' worth of food and supplies on hand at all times. We're just saying, "Instead of three days, why not 30 days? Why not 60 days?"

It's about starting off small. I got started by storing some canned goods in a few five-gallon buckets. I had a month's worth of food, and I felt pretty good. It was a natural progression from there to where I am today. After I had the food, I thought, "Well obviously I need water." From there, "Well how will I cook this food?" And, "What if it's winter and there is no heat?" And so on.

Getting people to simply start thinking about the "what-ifs" is key to helping them realize all of the things we need to survive, and how much of it is "provided" for us. If SHTF, our entire system of living is obsolete. It will go from, "If I sit at this desk and enter data into a spreadsheet for eight hours per day, I will get money that I can exchange for food, water, fuel, medical services, garbage removal, and everything else I never have to think about on a day-to-day basis." to, "If I don't already have this, or if I can't find it, my family will die soon." Helping somebody come to this realization on their own is leaps and bounds more productive than aggressively preaching it at them.

Getting people to start their own prepping efforts can be a lot of work. It involves teaching, demonstrating, helping, and otherwise spending your time to work with them. For some, all you have to do is "show them the light" and they will go full-speed ahead on their own. For others, they will look to you as a mentor of sorts. This may include showing them what you've done, how you did it, and how they can do it too. It's important that they go at their own pace and according to their resources. But you should be there to continue giving them a gentle nudge in the right direction.

People who have embraced prepping after being introduced to it by you are very likely to be interested in the idea of combining efforts with someone such as yourself. They can be a major asset to you, but you are the ultimate resource to them. And since you are the one who got them into prepping in the first place, you have the opportunity from square one to promote the community-based methodology.

Get involved with an online club or community of like-minded people

The key ingredient to a community is people. If you don't have any people, you have to find people. In a survival community, the ingredient you need is survivalists (as in, people who are committed to the idea of surviving). If you're still in need of prospective members after considering people you already know, you may have to look outside of people you already know. In short, this means making new friends!

The idea here is to find like-minded people. If you go out and try to meet new people with the intention of asking them to join your survival community, it's going to sound like, "Hey stranger, can I take you out into the woods to join my doomsday cult?" So it's best to stick with people who already believe in the importance of survival preparedness when seeking out people with whom you do not already have some sort of relationship.

One of the best ways to get to know new people is online! The enormous popularity of online dating is a testament to this. Talking with strangers online lets you engage in dialogue and get a pretty good feel for the sort of people they are. You can find out what are their beliefs, their practices, their intentions, and their motivations. You can get to know a person very well without ever having met them in "real life." There are people in my life who I have known for years and consider close friends, and I've never met them face-to-face.

As with real life, it's possible that you will encounter people with whom you do not want to be friends. As with real life, the internet has plenty of crazies and jerks. In the prepper and survivalist world, it's probable that you will encounter people from both extremes of the spectrum, from casual homesteading enthusiasts to full-on "tinfoil hat" doomsday conspiracists. Depending on your own beliefs, objectives, and personality, you can choose for yourself with whom you want to engage. If you start talking to somebody and it turns out that you don't like the cut of their jib, you can just move on. They don't know you, and you don't know them. However, if you meet the "right" kind of person for you, you can choose how far to take it and how fast.

As I mentioned, I've been "online friends" with a few guys for years. I would have absolutely no problem meeting them in real life and trusting them. They're good fellows. Unfortunately they live nowhere near the location of my survival retreat! This is an important factor. Part of the challenge of engaging with or meeting people online will be to find those who live within some reasonable proximity to you or your bug-out location (assuming you already have one). After a SHTF event, it will be difficult to travel very far. It's important that all members of your community can rendezvous at your retreat as soon as possible. I'm sure you all know by now that there is a huge online presence of preppers and survival enthusiasts. Finding a forum, chat room, or social media community of like-minded people shouldn't be incredibly difficult. Finding individuals who fit into your idea of an ideal "candidate," *and* who live somewhere nearby may be the challenging part.

Another option for engaging with like-minded people online is to create your own blog, forum, or group on a social media site. Start a Facebook group called "My State Community Prepping." Find a local prepping community on Reddit (there are lots!) or start your own. There are a lot of social media platforms, and there are a lot of preppers out there. It's just a matter of finding them!

Everybody is different, and every relationship progresses differently. It may only take weeks of chatting with somebody online before feeling comfortable enough to mention the subject of collaborating efforts. On the other hand, it could take years before that level of comfort and trust is established with somebody. The important thing is to make these connections, and to find these friends. A survival community doesn't work without a community!

Summary

One of the biggest challenges in organizing a survival community is finding the right people. When seeking potential members of your group, these are the best places to start:

- Preppers and/or survivalist you already know.
- Close friends and family who might be encouraged to start prepping.
- Online communities of like-minded people in your geographical area.

With other preppers, you don't need to convince them that being prepared is important. You only need to convince them that a community methodology is the way to go. Here are some "selling points" to consider when presenting this concept to fellow preppers:

- Describe the flaws in going it alone (security risks, too few people for the amount of necessary work, etc).
- Describe the benefits of a community (*Consolidation of Efforts* and *Compounding of Efforts*).
- Explain why you think he or she would be an important member of the community.
- Present the assets and resources already associated with the group:
    - Do you or another member already have land?
    - Are any assets already established (e.g., a well has been dug, a perimeter fence has been built, there is already a cabin and several outbuildings on the land)?

- What community-centric preps already exist (e.g., enough food to feed twenty people for five years has already been gathered and stored)?
- Is there already a rock-solid action plan for establishing and operating the retreat?
- Anything else that would instill confidence in a potential member that you are a group that has their stuff together and is committed to the initiative at hand.

For people who are not already prepping, you may be able to encourage them to start by helping them realize the importance of doing so. If you can get somebody on board, the concept of a community-based effort should be a very easy sell. When talking to people who are skeptical of prepping or any survivalist-type things, it can be challenging to coax them into having an open mind. Some key points to invite them to consider are:

- What would you do, specifically, if the power across the entire state went out for 24 hours?
- What if it went out for a week? Two weeks? A month?
- Where will you get food? How will you get to the place that might (emphasis on "might") have food?
- Where will water for drinking and cleaning come from?
- If it's winter, will you need heat?
- What happens when someone else decides that they want to take what you have so that *their* needs can be met?
- What do you think the majority of people in this state will do in that situation? Food lines? Large-scale displacement? Refugee camps? That's the best-case scenario. That's what happens when FEMA, the Red Cross, and the National Guard *is* deployable.
- What do you think people will do if there is no National Guard? What will happen when there is no rule of law? When bad people face no consequences for their actions, what are they capable of? When good people are watching their children slowly starve to death, what are *they* capable of? What would *you* do to feed your starving children?

Thomas Eddy

Once somebody starts to realize how reliant on "the system" they truly are for their most basic day-to-day needs, the wheels of thought start to turn. When those wheels start to turn, make sure you're there to help them get started on the right track.

Finding like-minded people on the internet is a viable option if you don't already know any prospective members for your community. Some ideas for places online to seek local preppers are:

- Prepping-specific community websites such as preppergroups.com.
- Non-specific club/organization portals such as meetup.com.
- Social networking websites like Facebook and Reddit.

Chapter 3
Establishing an Operational Plan

Whether or not you have completed the challenging task of assembling a full team of future community members, a comprehensive "game plan" must be drawn up. This should be done as far in advance as possible, given all circumstances and available resources. Plans can change and preparations can evolve, but an operational plan must be established and followed to achieve success.

Ideally, your team should consist of at least a dozen committed and dedicated adults who will plan, build, supply, and operate a survival retreat. However, if you don't yet have enough people on board it should not stop you from getting a plan put together with the people you *do* have. As I said, the operational plan can evolve and change as necessary if your team grows. But you have to start somewhere.

There is an awful lot that can go into putting together a survival retreat. The intricacies of each aspect of establishing such a thing are too vast to entirely cover in one book. This publication is intended to serve as a road map for putting the whole thing together, and will cover all of the major considerations that should be made. This chapter outlines the various aspects of planning that need to take place. Subsequent chapters will dive deeper into the specific areas of operation.

So what needs to get included in the plan? The answer is short but not simple: Anything and everything. How will you determine if it is time to bug out? Where will you rendezvous? What are the protocols for transporting people and supplies to the retreat? What are the very first things which must be done to "activate" the retreat after SHTF? What will be the specific day-to-day objectives and tasks during the first week? The first month? The first year and beyond?

Anything that *can* be planned *should* be planned. Of course not everything can be planned out to the finest detail, but the more you plan, the fewer variables there will be which can affect your probability of success. Every group's plan will look different, and will contain sections and details which are tailored to their specific objectives, assets, and resources. However, there are a few topics of particular importance which should be discussed and included in every group's operational plan.

A Team Effort

Whenever possible, the operational plan should be a concerted effort. That is to say, all current members of the group should be actively involved in crafting it. This is a team initiative that relies on a variety of skills, assets, and resources that each member is bringing to the table. This is not a situation where one person writes a manifesto that all others are expected to follow. Not only does the team owe it to one another to *act* like a team, the very reason you are a team is because everybody has different knowledge and skills. All ideas should be heard and discussed by the team.

It's likely that certain members will be better suited to craft certain components of the plan than others. For example, if one of your members is a former Army Ranger with advanced knowledge about base defenses and light-infantry combat tactics, he is probably the best person to take the lead on the section about retreat security. After he gets his thoughts down on paper, it should be presented to the group to discuss. If everybody is in agreement, add it to the operational plan!

Do you have an agriculturist on your team? It's probable that he or she is best suited to draft the section on food production. Do you have an engineer on your team? That person seems like an obvious choice to contribute to a section about building, maintenance, or overall logistics. It's only sensible that members take the lead on subjects in which they have relevant knowledge or expertise. Just keep in mind that the group as a whole must ultimately read, understand, discuss, and approve any item which gets added to the final operational plan.

Designing and Planning the Survival Retreat

This is where it all begins. This is where you and your team really get down to the nitty-gritty of figuring out all of the ins-and-outs of what your retreat will look like, where it will be, and how it will be equipped.

Current Assets and Resources

A great place to start is to write down all of the team's current assets and resources. This can include property that one of you already owns or is planning to acquire. It could include vehicles at your disposal, such as ATVs, boats, RVs, trucks, etc. Does anybody own any heavy equipment, such as a tractor or backhoe? Work on assembling an extensive list of such assets. Anything which can be used permanently at the retreat or can be transported to the retreat during bug-out should go on the list. Don't include items that you have no intention of using to benefit the retreat. Your sporty convertible isn't going to serve much purpose in the back-country, nor would you want it to! If it can be contributed to the cause, either now or when SHTF, write it down.

Your list of current assets and resources will hopefully be long. There should be various sections on your list. A few ideas for the types of sections your list should contain are:

- Land - Does someone already have land? If so, what assets or resources are already on that land?
- Vehicles - What vehicles do any of the members own which can be useful for either bugging out or for the operation of the retreat?
- Equipment - This can include tools, materials, and equipment that pertain specifically to prepping and living off-grid. Farm equipment, water purification, firearms, fishing supplies, and water containers are all examples of essential equipment. Big or small, we all have equipment that will be necessary or useful to our community.
- Established Preps - How much food and necessary supplies have already been prepared by each person? How much of it will be contributed to the group effort?
- Skills - Knowledge and experience are the ultimate assets! Which members have which skills? Who is an expert at what? Who is knowledgeable enough to be in charge of security? How about medical care? Agriculture? Construction? No matter how elaborately you have prepped, no other asset compares to knowledge and experience!
- Money - This is an obvious asset. Are the members capable of committing some cold, hard cash to the project? Everybody will contribute money in some way or another, often by using it to acquire more supplies. Building a survival retreat, and prepping in general, can be expensive projects. Figure out how much each person can contribute to the overall goals (upfront, each month, as-needed, etc). Some people

will be able to contribute more than others. Additionally, someone with few skills and no equipment can still be an asset, depending on how "prepared" their wallet is!

- Time - How much time is each person capable and willing to commit to establishing the community survival retreat? Again, some people may have more time they are able to contribute than others.

It's important that everybody contributes significantly. Some people will have more time than physical assets (money, equipment, etc). Some members have zero time but are willing to bankroll a significant portion of the project. It's possible that you will have a member who turns out to have zero time and zero physical assets to contribute. In such a case, you may want to consider whether or not that person will be an asset at all. Everybody must contribute! If that person happens to be an experienced field medic, soldier of fortune, mechanical engineer with a passion for farming, then he may be a major asset based on "skills" alone.

When your list is complete, it should contain anything and everything that currently exists which can be considered an asset or resource to establishing the survival community. The next thing to do is figure out your group's objectives. Once you have a list of current assets and a list of objectives, you can figure out where the gaps are. In other words, you can figure out what you still need to get and do in order to fulfill the group's objectives.

Community Objectives

When talking about a survival community, there is one ultimate objective: To live! But the details and interpretation of what it means to "live" may vary from group to group. Some groups may decide that they absolutely require some type of electrical capabilities. This would mean, of course, that their plan will have to involve a lot of considerations for power generation, such as solar or wind. Some groups may decide that their best course of action is to acquire food products that can be stored indefinitely, and rely solely on that stored food for sustenance. Other groups will make considerations for growing and/or raising their own food for the long-term. These are things which must be determined and written down by the group so that all efforts can be aligned toward the common goals.

Think about how many people your ideal community will support. How much water will need to be stored? How will it be stored? How much room for agriculture is needed? What sort of land will that require? Will your land be near a lake or river? How does that affect what your community is capable of? Will each family have their own living quarters, or will there be a communal structure? What sort of security measures are needed?

Whether or not you already have the location of your future retreat, you should begin creating a map of sorts. Figure out where everything will go. Living quarters (whether that means cabins, tents, RVs, or something else), storage facilities for supplies, food prep area, one or more outhouses, a well for water - these are just a few examples of the facilities which should be planned and plotted out on a map.

Anything and everything that needs to get established before your retreat is operational must be considered. Once you know your objectives, you can determine what is needed to reach them. Once you know what you need, where it will go, and how it will be achieved, you can determine what you still need to acquire and what you still need to learn.

What is Still Needed

It's guaranteed that you will discover a great number of things that are still needed before your survival retreat can be considered "operational." There are bound to be a lot of assets and resources as a starting point any time a group of dedicated preppers get together, but in most cases there will be a ton of work to do and materials to get before everything is ready.

The longer you prep, the more your wish list of skills and supplies will grow. The inevitability of this can make it somewhat impossible to draft a truly complete list of everything you still need. Nevertheless, start by considering your group's current list of objectives, and work towards them.

Some amenities for the retreat will be simple. If an objective is to have an area dedicated to chopping wood, all you really need is a chopping block, cutting tools, and the space to put it all. It shouldn't be too hard to figure out a good place for that area, and it's certainly not difficult to figure out what materials and tools are needed. On the other hand, some features of the retreat may be far more complex, and will require a lot more planning, materials, and labor. Digging a well, constructing an outbuilding, putting up a perimeter fence - These examples all require significant planning, resources, and time to complete. Each "thing" that you want your retreat to have will be another page in your extensive Operational Plan, and each will surely contribute several lines to your "What is Still Needed?" list.

Aside from features of the retreat itself, there are the supplies with which the retreat will be stocked. Food, water, and everything else must be stocked for (at least) the first several months of operation. That's a lot of stuff! How many bags of rice will be needed to feed the amount of people you expect to support? How many jars, buckets, or Mylar bags will be needed to store that rice? Each person requires a minimum of one gallon of clean water per day. One gallon per person multiplied by twenty people comes out to over 7,000 gallons of clean water you should aim to store, at the minimum. How will it be stored? What kind of containers will you use? How many containers will be needed? Where will the water come from? Does it need to be purified first? What will that entail? Does it need an additive/preservative?

This list is going to be long if you're doing it right. Start broad, and work your way down. Break up your retreat's needs by category of necessity. For example, "Heat" is a category. How will you account for heat in the cold months? What is needed for warmth to be provided to all members of the community? Another category may be "Sanitation". What is needed for the community to operate in a sanitary way? This includes plans for a latrine/outhouse, as well as cleaning of food prep equipment. How will wastewater be disposed of? How will you wash your hands? What supplies or materials do you need to accomplish this? Consider everything you want to be able to do in your retreat, and then consider a backup/alternative way to do each of those things. What are the supplies, materials, equipment, and skills that you will need to make all of those things happen?

Operating as a Club or Legitimate Organization

Depending on the nature of your relationship with the other members of your group, and depending on the assets and resources the individual members are capable of contributing, you might consider organizing your group as an official club. This may involve bylaws and/or legal documents that outline each member's position or "stake" in the club's assets. If you consider it important to do so, you can have everything outlined in legally-binding documents. These documents can lay out things like asset allocation should a member leave or if the group dissolves altogether. Every group is different, and particularly if the monetary contributions from members are quite lop-sided, some consider it wise to protect themselves and their investments. It may not seem to coincide with the spirit of a survivalist community, but remember that we're talking about folks who live their lives around the concept of being prepared for the worst!

Organizing your group as a club doesn't have to involve legal contracts and "pre-nuptial agreements," if you will. Some groups operate in a way that requires a certain amount of time or monetary commitment per month (or year, or however they decide to set it up). One group I am familiar with requires a relatively large initial "buy-in" from their members, and also substantial annual dues. This is a well-established group with a very elaborate retreat setup, and is comprised of somewhat well-to-do people. If you can afford it, almost anyone can join.

I don't necessarily recommend requiring each member to "buy in" with an initial cash contribution, but I don't think that some sort of monthly or annual dues is a terrible idea. The initial members of your group should come to an agreement on this, and determine how a dues schedule should be structured. Dues can be monetary, or perhaps members' individual contributions to the project can be considered towards their dues owed. In some cases, perhaps time/labor could be considered towards dues. I'd hate to exclude a hard working person with all the time and dedication in the world just because he doesn't have a lot of cash to throw around. Again, your group should decide such things on a case-by-case basis. Even if you don't want to somehow incorporate yourselves as a legitimate "club", you should spend some time to decide what is expected of each member, and what will happen if disputes arise regarding any of the group's members or contributions.

Organizational Structure

However your group decides to organize itself, it is wise to come to an agreement on the leadership structure and "diplomatic process". If there is to be an hierarchy in leadership, it must be established from day one. If the group is 100% democratic, then it must be determined how that will work. If voting on an issue, will a simple majority pass? Must it be unanimous? What if there is a tie? Figure out what sort of things you are likely to need a vote on (accepting new members, spending group funds, choosing an operational process, etc), and settle on the protocol for how it must be handled. Rigid organization and adherence to your own established by-laws is absolutely essential to keeping your community glued together.

Read more about organizational structures, leadership, and member roles in Chapter 8.

Bugging-Out

Possibly the most daunting stage of planning your survival community will involve the initial establishment of the retreat itself. Whether or not you've completed actually creating and supplying the retreat, you need to have a plan for what to do if it's time to bug-out. Ideally, your retreat will be "ready to rock" long before it's truly needed. It's possible, of course, that the time to "head for the hills" may come while you're still in the middle of setting it up. Building a survival compound is no easy task, and may take years. Either way, a plan must be made for the bug-out procedure, as well as initial "activation" of the retreat no matter what stage of preparedness you happen to be at.

Read more about bugging out in Chapter 6.

Activation of Retreat and Short-Term Operation

If nobody is living at your retreat throughout the year, things likely to be in a state of dormancy much of the time. Systems are tested and procedures are practiced, but for much of the time, most of the retreat is considered "deactivated". The plumbing is winterized. Any electrical appliances are unplugged. Everything is stowed and secured in a way that will resist weather, animals, and vandals for the periods of time when members of the group are not present. Everything is simply...waiting. Should the time ever come, the entire retreat is ready and waiting to be "activated".

After you've successfully bugged out and activated the retreat, what's next? The initial days or weeks that your survival retreat is operational will look a bit different than the months or years that may follow. In the beginning, it's quite likely that uncertainty will surround the situation which caused you to bug out in the first place. It's probable that things in "civilized society" will normalize and go back to the status quo before terribly long. During this time, and until your group is quite certain that you're going to be in this for the long haul, it makes sense to operate your retreat in a "short-term" capacity. If it's possible that in a couple weeks you may find out that everything is going to be OK, it stands to reason that you will deactivate the retreat and head back to your normal lives. It's just good sense to run at "partial capacity" for the first little while, until you are 100% sure that the community is staying put for the long-term.

Long-Term Operation

If all signs point to this societal breakdown being an indefinite thing, you'll want to initiate your long-term plan. It may be obvious as soon as you bug out, depending on the severity of the event which caused you to bug out in the first place. Regardless of when you make the call that you are in a long-term survival situation, making that call should trigger your long-term plan. This tends to mean planting vegetables, hunting/trapping game, and otherwise preparing to operate in a sustainable way as your stored goods will be eventually depleted.

Read more about retreat activation, short-term, and long-term operation in Chapter 7.

Finding/Accepting New Members Down the Road

Perhaps one of the riskiest and most complicated aspects of operating your community after SHTF is the prospect of accepting new members. Needless to say, it's going to be difficult to have any level of trust for a person you've never met in a post-SHTF environment. It will be difficult to know if somebody is being genuine or if they are perpetrating an elaborate manipulation. Desperate people are capable of anything. Some may bring a gun and try to take what you have by force. Others may try to weasel their way into your circle through deception and acting. It's a very tricky business determining if you should allow someone in, be it for a meal and some fresh water or as a permanent new member.

Read more about new members after SHTF in Chapter 15.

Summary

Building a survival retreat is an enormous project. There are countless variables, specifications, and requirements which need to get figured out in advance by your group. Anything that *can* be planned for *should* be planned for. If your operational plan is done right, it will be very long. When your group gets together to assemble the operational plan for your community, the following should be considered:

Every essential member of your community should be involved in creating the plan:
- Some members may be in charge of crafting certain aspects of the plan, based on their expertise or skill set.

- Regardless of which members physically write each piece of the plan, all members must read, understand, and agree upon all parts.

When setting out to create your group's operational plan, start by figuring out these key things:

- Current assets and resources - Materials, skills, and knowledge that the members currently possess and can contribute to the objective.
- Community objectives - What do you want to have, and what do you want to achieve as a community?
- What is still needed - You know what you have, and you know what you want. What items, skills, or knowledge do you still need in order to reach the community objectives?
- Incorporation - Should your members form a legitimate club or corporation to make sure everyone is covered from a legal standpoint?
- Organizational structure - How will the hierarchy of leadership and diplomatic process in your community be structured?

Bugging Out and Retreat Activation:

- What is your team's plan for bugging out? If not the retreat itself, where is your rendezvous point?
- Each member should individually consider their own plan for "closing up shop" when they must leave their home.
- Activating the retreat after SHTF should be done according to a rigid procedure. Each member should know exactly what their role is during activation, and during the short-term operation of the retreat.

Long-Term Operation:

- How will you handle food production such as raising animals, growing vegetables, or hunting?
- How will you continue to improve perimeter security?
- What other considerations must be made for your retreat to operate as a full-fledged, sustainable homestead once short-term supplies and resources begin to dwindle?

Dealing with Newcomers:
- Will your community accept new members after SHTF?
- What will be the protocol to accept and acclimate newcomers?
- How will the community handle a stranger who is *not* welcome?

Chapter 4
Choosing an Ideal Location for Your Retreat

The community-based methodology for prepping revolves entirely around the idea of having a physical location where the members of your survival group will assemble if society begins to unravel. While many prepping methodologies involve "bugging-in" at your primary residence, this book means to discuss the establishment and operation of a bug-out location. This chapter is all about choosing the best possible location for your survival retreat.

If a member of your group already owns a remote piece of land, this chapter may not be as relevant for you. Even if it's not the absolutely perfect land or location, already having that location eliminates an enormous hurdle that most will have to face. The land you currently have is better than any land you don't!

If you and your group have yet to procure a remote property, there are a few important criteria to consider when you begin your search. Obviously affordability will factor in above all else. That is to say, our aim is to acquire the best possible piece of land that is within our physical capability of purchasing. That being said, here are some essential criteria to think about when setting out to plan the location for your survival retreat.

Inaccessibility

It surely goes without saying that one of the most essential characteristics of your retreat's location is that it is far away from heavily (or even moderately) populated areas. Other people will become your greatest threat, so it's a no-brainer that Priority #1 is to get away from other people!

Depending on your geographical region, the remote location for your camp is probably going to fit somewhere within one of these categories:

- Woods/forest
- Farmland/plains
- Desert
- Coastal/island

Whichever landscape you choose, make sure it's far enough off the beaten path that your camp won't be the first rest stop on the ravaging horde's road trip of destruction.

Accessibility

While it's of the utmost importance to build your retreat as close to "the middle of nowhere" as you can, it's equally important that all of your members can physically get there.

I love the idea of trekking to the furthest reaches of civilization and setting up the ultimate compound that no one could ever possibly find. But it's just not realistic. Not only would it be incredibly difficult to regularly visit the property in order to develop the retreat, but it would be next to impossible to actually get there if civilization has begun to fall apart. If it takes 3 hours on the freeway to drive somewhere right now, how long will it take to get there when the main roads are gridlocked and chaotic?

Choosing the perfect spot for your retreat will be a fine balancing act of "far enough away that most people will never know it's there" and "close enough that we can all actually get there in a realistic amount of time."

Also regarding accessibility, will all of your members be able to traverse the terrain that separates them from the retreat? We'd all love to construct a fortress atop a mountain, but most of us don't have helicopters or jet-packs with which to access it. A remote island would certainly have its perks, but everybody must have a boat to get there. And not only should they have a way, they should have a backup way. Locations that are deep in the woods or up in the hills may require a vehicle with high ground clearance and possibly four-wheel drive.

Wherever you decide to establish your camp, just be sure that the geographic location and the terrain allow for all members of your community to realistically get there in one piece.

Climate

While this book could serve as a useful roadmap for anyone looking to establish a bug-out retreat, it's certainly geared towards people living in the United States. That being said, the U.S. is a vast place that encompasses many different climate zones and geographic regions. Each have their pros and cons when thinking about where to set up shop.

Thomas Eddy

Northern States

The Northwestern, Northeastern, and Midwestern states offer an incredibly vast array of remote landscapes with an abundance of natural resources. From the mountains of Montana to the forests of New England, and everything in between, people in these regions have near-countless options when searching for land on which to establish a bug-out location.

There are plenty of positive aspects about living off-grid in a northern or central climate zone. Natural resources like timber, fresh water, and fertile land are plentiful. The warmer seasons are accommodating to growing crops, and keeping livestock is entirely doable year-round. In nearly every state within these regions, you should be able to find the type of landscape that suits your requirements, whether it's wide-open farmland or deep woods.

Obviously one of the biggest challenges with running an off-grid camp in a northern state is going to be winter. Crops don't grow in the winter, accommodations must be made for livestock in the cold months, and gathering enough firewood for the season costs a lot of effort. Cold weather and snow can also hinder travel, and make things like fishing and hunting more difficult. On the other hand, cold temperatures present the capability to store fresh meat and other food for a longer period of time.

Southeastern States

Much like in the north, states in the southeastern U.S. are plentiful with farmland, forests, and other remote locations. The deep south probably has as many "remote" parts as it does populated parts. The variety of critters for hunting, fresh water sources, and remote areas make this region a somewhat popular destination for preppers and survivalists.

An obvious perk to living in a southern state is that winters are not particularly brutal and cold. As somebody who was born and raised in a northern state, I don't personally consider this to be that big of an advantage, but it certainly eliminates the very real concern of freezing to death. The biggest advantage to operating a homestead in a southeastern state, in my opinion, is that vegetables can be grown during much more of the year.

The biggest disadvantage to living in the deep south, also according to my opinion, is the prevalence of vermin and pests. Because the weather is hospitable for most of the year to creatures big and small, rodents and insects can be a major problem. Disease-carrying rats may infest your food stocks. Cockroaches could run rampant in damp, dark places. Mosquitoes will do their best to suck you dry during most parts of the year. This may not be a terrible concern for folks who are from Mississippi or Arkansas, but the bugs and vermin are enough to keep this Northern boy well above the freeze line!

Southwestern States

The Southwest region of the U.S. is surely, by all reasonable criteria, the least hospitable environment for a homesteading lifestyle. While there are plenty of folks who have lived off the land in places like New Mexico and Arizona, it takes a special skill-set and knowledgebase to survive in such a region. I'd say that it also takes a somewhat strong passion for the region itself, as those who decide to homestead in those states surely recognize the difficulties in doing so when compared with other regions.

The arid climate and desert landscape present serious challenges, such as availability of fresh water, timber, and abundance of wild game animals. While the desert is enormous, much of the region simply isn't accommodating to a purely off-grid lifestyle. For those who will bug-out to locations in the Southwestern states, they will not be heading to a camp set up in wide-open desert. This limits the number of physically-viable locations in which communities can be set up which are remote enough, protected enough, and resource-rich enough. It's true that you can go pretty far off the radar when you head into desert country, but that's not going to do much good unless you also have a means of providing water, food, and other necessities.

The vast, arid landscape of the Southwestern United States is not a place that I would personally recommend for any group looking to set up a survival retreat. Homesteading in this region would present constant challenges due to the scarcity of water, the infertile land, and the unforgiving terrain.

Alaska

See the previous section about Northern states, and kick it up a notch! Alaska can be the best or the worst place for an off-grid bug-out location. The winters are relentless and wicked, but the resources are plentiful. Much of the state is incredibly remote wilderness, but getting there (before or after SHTF) can be a serious challenge.

The wilds of Alaska may seem like the "Holy Grail" of bug-out locations. I think this may be true, but only for people who live out there for a very long time. Many families have lived in the boonies of Alaska for generations, and they know what it takes to survive in such a place. Alaska isn't a place for "part-timers". It's the sort of place where you go all-in or not at all.

Hawaii (and Other Island Territories)

Since I talked about all of the regions of the continental United states and Alaska, I figured I'd better mention Hawaii. The climate is wonderful year-round, the volcanic soil is fertile, and a tropical island is pretty darn remote. Nevertheless, Hawaii is a terrible place to be stranded if SHTF!

Like any populated island sitting in the middle of an ocean, I would never recommend Hawaii as a place to hole-up when the framework of society begins tumbling down. It may have been a very long time ago, but Hawaii is not a self-sufficient place. Nearly everything that residents of the islands consume has to be shipped in from the mainland. Sure, you can't get much more remote than "A thousand miles into the ocean," but it's still a very populated place. The residents of the islands are still going to be competing for food and resources once the supply chain stops. When that happens, being in Hawaii will be as good as being trapped in a small cage full of hungry wolves.

For those who currently live in Hawaii and are serious about forming a survival community and establishing a bug-out retreat, my advice to you is, "Move."

Natural Resources

I touched on the topic of natural resources a little bit in the "Climate" section above, but it's a subject that's important enough to warrant a deeper dive. Wherever you choose to establish your retreat, in whichever region you decide, the success or failure of your survival hinges upon the availability of resources. Initially, many of your resource requirements can be fulfilled by utilizing your stored preps. It's possible to store years' worth of food and supplies. Storing a decade of supplies for 20+ people is an enormous undertaking and incredible expense, but it can be done.

But what if you need more than ten years of supplies? What if you add more members to your group after SHTF? What if some of your supplies get compromised by weather, pests, or human error? What if you end up needing things that you hadn't planned for?

There are only three ways to get what you need when the supply chain doesn't exist:

- Already have it
- Scavenge it
- Grow/build/gather it

This section is all about the "grow/build/gather" option. We already talked about utilizing your preexisting preps. Scavenging is an invaluable method for getting what you need, but it comes with a lot of risks. It involves traveling, and it will take you to traces of civilization where the odds of running into strangers are much higher. Scavenging will almost certainly be a necessity in some cases, but it's not going to keep you fed, hydrated, and sheltered indefinitely.

You need food? You will either need to grow it, hunt it, or gather it. Need to build a new structure or repair an existing one? I'm afraid Home Depot isn't an option. Nature is going to be your hardware store. You'll need lots of water for drinking, cleaning, and gardening.

Thomas Eddy

When considering a plot of land for your survival retreat, you must ask this question: "Will the natural resources around this location be enough to provide for our basic needs?"

As I've said before, every group's requirements will differ. But here are some examples of what my group considered to be essential natural resources when planning the location of our retreat:

Water

Arguably the most essential of all resources, a near-unlimited supply of fresh water is absolutely vital. A human being needs a minimum of about one gallon of water per day. This estimate takes into account what is needed for hydration, as well as that one person's water needs for cooking and cleaning over the course of one day.

There are three main sources for fresh water when you are off the grid: Rain, groundwater, and bodies of water (such as lakes, rivers, streams, ponds, etc.). It's important to know which of these will be available to you wherever you decide to establish your retreat.

Trees

There is nothing more beautiful than a tree! Trees play such an important role in fulfilling several of our most basic needs. They provide lumber for building shelter. They provide firewood for keeping warm, cooking, and purifying water. They provide habitats for various animals that we can harvest for food. When you have lots of them in one place, they provide natural security and concealment.

In certain climate zones, it's possible to get by without having an abundance of trees nearby. In the Southwestern states you could build adobe structures, and burning wood for heat isn't nearly as important. But in my humble opinion, anywhere that's worth living will have trees as far as the eye can see! If you have a forest outside your door, you have a lifetime of priceless resources.

Game Animals/Fish

Meat's back on the menu, boys! Unless you are a very serious and skilled horticulturist, living a vegetarian lifestyle in an off-grid/post-SHTF situation is going to be close to impossible. For most of us, our protein source will be meat. And there's no better or fresher meat than the kind you harvest yourself.

The prevalence of game animals and/or fish near your location will very possibly mean the difference between life and death in a long-term survival scenario. When there is no protein left to eat from your stored goods, nature will be your grocery store. Be sure to know what types of wild game and fish can be found in the location you choose. Get familiar with all manner of big game, small game, fowl, and fish.

Fertile Soil

This one is pretty self-explanatory. In order to grow plants, you need fertile soil. You can make a nutrient-rich substrate from various components if your existing earth isn't particularly fertile, but it's sure easier if you have some great dirt to work with from the get-go. In either case, the success of your garden depends on this natural resource. You either need existing soil that is rich and fertile, or you need the ingredients that can be used to create it.

Read more about hunting and gardening in Chapter 9.
Read more about fulfilling your community's off-grid water demands in Chapter 10.
Read more about firewood in Chapter 11.

Security Advantages

When considering a location for your survival retreat, you must constantly think about what factors will contribute to the success (or failure) of your group's survival. When there is no such thing as law enforcement, and your group is alone and isolated, security will be among your greatest concerns. So set yourself up for success by choosing a location that provides any number of natural security advantages.

When looking at a plot of land, ask yourself, "Does the landscape provide for any tactical protection against security threats?" If you're looking at a forty-acre parcel of wide-open farmland that is surrounded by another few hundred acres of wide-open farmland, you can probably assume that the land doesn't offer much in the way of natural security advantages.

What kinds of natural features should you look for? Anything and everything could be looked at from a security standpoint, but here is a short list of features to keep an eye out for:

High Ground

It's better to be looking down upon your enemy than looking up. It's one of the most fundamental strategic advantages. Having the "high ground" allows you to see threats better than threats can see you. Thanks to gravity, holding a position atop a hill makes it easier for you to access a threat while making it harder for the threat to access you. While a gang of pillagers are trudging up the hill towards your camp, you're securing the gates and getting into defensive positions because you saw them coming a mile away. And if you happen to have the Temple of Doom's architect working with your team, you can always roll an enormous stone ball down to the advancing marauders!

Cover

In my ideal bug-out situation, nobody would have any idea that my retreat exists unless they already know it exists. Aside from the provision of natural resources, the main reason I prefer a heavily-wooded landscape for my camp is that it's almost impossible to see unless you're at it or immediately next to it. Some wayward traveler could be hiking through the woods within a couple hundred feet of my perimeter, and they'd never have any idea unless a sound or smell gave it away. To take it a step further, the camp is nearly entirely obstructed from above due to tree cover. I appreciate this because even Google Earth satellite pictures don't reveal anything of interest to prying eyes

(Though this part is a bit more relevant *before* the collapse of civilization).

To contrast the deep concealment of a heavily wooded area, imagine a lone farmhouse floating in a sea of prairie. A hungry cutthroat or a desperate mob will see this as soon as they round the horizon. There are advantages to establishing a homestead out in wide-open country, but security via concealment and cover isn't one of them. When it comes to the topic of being visible to potential threats, you might as well name the retreat "Camp Sitting Duck". However, if your group is very large or you have the resources to construct elaborate security features, farmland could be a viable option.

Natural Perimeter

The primary directive of any stronghold is to keep unwanted visitors out of it. All of your hard work, as well as your lives, are at risk if unwelcome people or animals are able to access the inner sanctum of your retreat. And nothing keeps out trespassers better than a wall. Call it a fence, a wall, or a perimeter; I'm talking about a physical barrier between the inside of your camp and the rest of the outside world. The most important thing to know is that you need one.

That being said, constructing a wall or fence is a ton of work. It requires a lot of resources. I know from experience that building even a simple privacy fence in a residential back yard entails a lot of grueling labor and expensive materials. The perimeter around your retreat needs to be taller, thicker, and stronger than the average backyard fence. So any help that Mother Nature can provide with this, I will embrace with open arms! When looking for your ideal retreat location, keep an eye out for any natural features which can contribute to your camp's security perimeter.

What sort of natural features should you look for? Here are just a few ideas:
- Cliff wall or drop-off - If your camp borders a cliff, this is an obvious barrier which would prevent someone from walking or driving into your camp. If you are at the top of the cliff, it would be very difficult for someone to gain access from below because it would involve climbing

straight up. If you are at the bottom of a cliff, your camp will back up to an enormous wall and the only way to gain access from that side would be dropping straight down.

- Shoreline - Having your camp border a body of water can have incredible advantages from a resources perspective. It can offer security advantages too, if the body of water is wide enough that a person could not traverse it on foot. However, relying on a shoreline alone can also leave you very vulnerable, should someone with a boat and bad intentions stumble upon your retreat.

- Tree line - This goes back to the "deep woods" concept that I am so fond of. Being surrounded on all sides by thick forest offers concealment/cover for your camp, but it could also offer cover for bad people who are interested in sneaking up on you. This is why the trees alone aren't enough, and you need that physical barrier. The most important part of a fence is the posts. They bear the weight and provide the structure. Well, if your location is surrounded by trees, you have bigger, stronger, and more numerous fence posts than you could ever hope to install yourself! You can use the trees in the construction of your perimeter wall. You just have to fill in the gaps (with timber, chain link, sheet metal, etc).

Escape Route

Deep cover and natural perimeters can be invaluable for helping to keep unwanted guests away from your compound. But what happens if, despite your best efforts, strangers with bad intentions manage to find and access your location? Could those natural security features suddenly become a dangerous trap?

Having your retreat back up to a cliff wall would provide an incredible border on at least one side, but what sort of havoc could be wreaked if some unsavory characters were positioned atop that cliff? Could they push heavy objects over the edge? Could they drop ropes and rappel straight into your camp? At the very least, they would have the unquestionable higher ground in a standoff.

Or what if your retreat is positioned at the top of that cliff and you are being advanced upon from the other side? Unless you have rappel lines all set to go, you're effectively trapped against the very drop-off that served as protection up to that point.

How about a lake? Can you escape by boat if the front gates of your compound have been breached? If you have a tall and rigid wall around your entire location, do you have an alternate way to get out should the main entrance become compromised?

It's the same point that I make time and again: No matter how solid your Plan A, you need to prepare a Plan B. No matter what natural security advantages your location offers, you have to make sure that you don't become trapped like fish in a barrel should your retreat become faced with a terrible threat.

Read more about retreat security in Chapter 14.

Existing Amenities

Let's be realistic: Constructing a survival retreat on a remote piece of land is going to be expensive. It's going to cost a lot of time, or it's going to cost a lot of money. Depending on how elaborate you make it, it may cost an awful lot of both. So why not make it easier on yourself, if possible? Finding a retreat location that has already been outfitted with useful amenities means one or more fewer things that you need to acquire, install, build, etc.
When you're considering a piece of property, be sure to closely identify and examine anything that someone else has already established. Does the property have any existing structures, buildings, or infrastructure which may be useful?

On a lot of remote land parcels in my state, you'll find a hunting cabin or small house. It's quite common for acreage to have a large pole-barn on it, constructed by a previous owner. You will often find a well already dug, or a septic tank already buried. Perhaps these features were for an old home which has been demolished. Oftentimes such features will be put in by a landowner who intended to build a home or other building, but for some reason didn't end up doing so.

For every cabin, house, or outbuilding the property already comes with, it's one less cabin, house, or outbuilding that you have to construct. It could mean one less well to dig, or one less septic tank to install.

Many vacant land parcels are set up to be connected to the municipal power grid, should someone ever come along and decide to build on it. While this wouldn't do much good for your community after SHTF, having electric service could be quite welcome in the meantime. Building and developing your retreat will sure be a lot easier if you can plug in your power tools and other appliances, and it's cheaper to use municipal power than to buy gasoline for generators. And even after the retreat is established, uninterrupted electricity is a wonderful luxury to have (at least until the day comes when the juice stops flowing). Depending on how remote your retreat is, having the capability of connecting to municipal power is a feature worth considering.

Depending on just how remote your property is, there may be limited road access or no road access at all. If you purchase a tract of wooded land that does not have its own road, you may have to rely on an easement from a neighboring property. Not only can such arrangements cause problems between neighbors, but I don't like the idea of a neighboring landowner getting into my business when they see various vehicles, people, and equipment coming and going across their property at any/all times. It seems like a simple thing, but I recommend that your land is not locked between other parcels, and you have your own path to and from the main road.

Summary

For those who don't already have a piece of land on which to establish their retreat, selecting a suitable location is perhaps the most important and most daunting step in your journey to establishing a survival community. Acquiring a remote piece of property is a big investment, and it represents a big commitment. If you and/or your group are going to take this massive step towards the ultimate goal of surviving and thriving during uncertain and dangerous times, you owe it to yourselves to do your homework in order to find the most advantageous and well-suited parcel of land.

Before you even begin to start shopping for property, your group must determine these important factors:

Which type of landscape is best suited to help fulfill the long-term objectives of your group?

- Woods/forest
- Farmland/plains
- Desert
- Coastal/island

In which region/climate zone will the retreat be located?

- Northeastern, Northwestern, or Midwestern
- Southeastern
- Southwestern
- Alaska
- Hawaii (or other island territories)

Is there an abundance of natural resources in the vicinity of your location?

- Fresh water
- Trees and other plant life
- Game animals or fish
- Fertile soil

Thomas Eddy

Does the location offer any naturally-occurring security advantages?

- High Ground
- Cover/concealment
- Natural perimeter
- Escape options

Does the property you are considering already have any useful amenities or infrastructure?

- Cabin/house
- Barn or other outbuildings
- Well, pump, or plumbing
- Septic tank/field
- Municipal electric service
- Road/trail access

Chapter 5
Building and Prepping Your Retreat

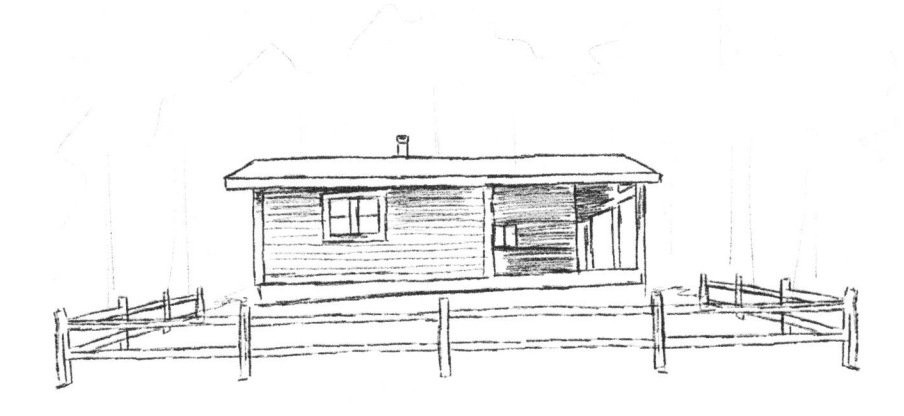

If you or the other members in your group have vast financial resources, you can probably go out and buy a fully-furnished, fully-functional off-grid "resort" that somebody else has taken the time and energy to build. Some people purchase decommissioned missile silos and recondition them to serve as a doomsday survival bunker. I've seen realty listings on the internet for elaborate properties that include multiple buildings, backup power sources, and all other manner of off-grid self-sufficiency. For a hefty price tag, you too can likely find an amazing property that is already setup to be the survival retreat of your dreams.

But this isn't realistic for most of us. If you're like me, and don't have millions of dollars burning a hole in your vault, you'll need to take more of a DIY approach. Setting up a survival retreat will take years, and it's the sort of project that you'll have a hard time ever considering "complete". Just like prepping at home, we all have an objective. But by the time we get there, we've thought of a better way to do something, or realized a different thing altogether that we need to be setting up. It's just the sort of thing that is never really finished. And that's OK.

As I've said a dozen times in this book so far, there is no one "correct" way to go about this. My primary aim is to outline the types of things that must be considered. There is not a "one size fits all" solution to establishing and stocking a survival retreat. Ultimately, your group must decide what it needs, and how resources will be allocated in order to make that happen. Depending on your climate, size of group, and long-term objectives, your camp may take a very different shape and size than that of any other group. This section is all about figuring out what your group requires in a retreat and what it will take to get there.

Size of Property

As I said in the last chapter, the best piece of property is the one you already have. Therefore, if you already have the land, then the space you have to work with has already been dictated. Planning the layout of your retreat within the parameters of physical space before you just makes sense.

If you have yet to acquire land, you will need to determine how much space you need. I'll always recommend getting as big of a plot as your group can afford. The more space (and natural resources) that surrounds your camp, the better. Keep in mind that you don't have to use your entire piece of land for the "inner circle" of your compound. Just make sure that there is enough space to put everything that your group has decided it needs. Remember that the bigger your compound, the bigger the perimeter that you have to secure.

Buildings/Structures

For most of us, an effective survival retreat will include at least a couple of structures. I'm sure a successful camp could be operated without any permanent buildings, depending on the climate, available natural resources, and requirements of the group involved. But for a long-term homesteading scenario, permanent structures will make a world of difference when it comes to both comfort and survivability.

When planning what kind of structures you may need, you have to think about all of the various needs that will have to be met. Some of the needs are obvious. You need shelter from the weather. You need a barrier to keep out animals. You need a safe and dry place to store food and supplies. In many cases, one structure can serve multiple purposes. Depending on your group and your resources, you may be able to get away with having a single building.

it's all about figuring out what you *need* to do in order to survive and be successful, and then figuring out what it will take to accomplish that according to your group's capabilities and preferences. Here is a list of common purposes for which buildings/structures can be necessary:

- Sleeping/living quarters
- Food prep/eating
- Food/supplies storage
- Tools/equipment storage
- Lavatory/hygiene
- Common area/gathering place
- Security headquarters/armory
- Barn/chicken coop

For one family running a homestead, it's quite common for them to have a single house or cabin. This lone building would serve as the sleeping area, kitchen, storage unit, and just about everything in-between. Toss in a small barn or chicken coop, and it can work. This is how families lived for hundreds of years, after all!

But in line with the community-based methodology, your retreat will not be inhabited by just a single family unit. The idea here is to create a place that will accommodate a couple dozen people, or more. For that many people to be healthy, happy, and safe your operation will likely need to be scaled up a bit from the "lone cabin in the woods" setup. Remember that this is meant to be a place where many people may live and grow indefinitely. A good rule of thumb is "Don't go bigger than you need, but don't go smaller than you need." In other words: It would save a lot of time and resources to create your operational plan around the idea that twenty people will live, work, eat, clean, and play in a single home, but it's not realistic and it doesn't make for a happy and healthy group of people.

So what does this mean? For my group, it meant that we had to plan and build multiple structures in our camp. We determined that in order to meet our objectives of creating a place that would comfortably sustain us and our families indefinitely, and according to the financial and physical resources available to us, we needed to construct a number of buildings. It didn't happen all at once, and it is in fact still ongoing. As time and funds permit, we make some more progress towards the overall goal according to our operational plan. That's how it goes, and we consider it to be a pretty normal and realistic progression.

> In order to equip you with plenty of ideas to consider, I'll outline the basic layout of my group's retreat. To help visualize how a survival compound may be setup, let's look at a breakdown of structures, systems/infrastructure, and the land itself.
>
> Keep in mind that my group has spent many years and devoted a lot of resources to building our retreat. It's come to be a place that our families consider a private getaway, and not just a survival compound. Additionally, two members of the group are husband and wife retirees who now live there full time. Treating it as a retirement destination, hunting camp, and

vacation property that will be passed down to future generations helps in justifying the effort and expense that we have collectively chosen to devote to its development. I recognize that our retreat is somewhat elaborate, and it is not reflective of what every prepper group is going to have the capability to create. Nevertheless, I believe there is value in sharing what we have done in order to provide several ideas and considerations that should be explored.

The Land

Our retreat is situated near the center of an approximately 80 acre parcel of wooded land. The enclosed section of the property that is considered the "compound" occupies an area of about 3 acres. It has been mostly cleared of trees and brush. A small stream runs through the property, although not within the compound's perimeter. The stream is roughly 150 yards away from the northwest corner of the perimeter.

A section of the compound has been designated specifically for gardening. Not quite a quarter acre, this area is partitioned into smaller sections to grow various vegetables and herbs. A simple irrigation system runs throughout the garden, and is sourced from the rainwater catchment system that is attached to the main structures.

Buildings/Structures

When my group acquired our land, the only existing structure was a tiny, dilapidated home. While the house itself could not be salvaged, its accompanying well and septic tank were intact. This bit of existing infrastructure was a most welcome, as it ended up saving a lot of time, effort, and money.

In the absence of any dwelling or other structure, we had a mostly blank slate to work with. We already knew how many people/families the retreat needed to accommodate, and we had already decided as a group what our long-term objectives were. As a group, we decided the standards by which we want to live. Accordingly, the blueprint for our compound came together.

Within the compound there are 11 buildings:

Dwellings

There are 5 cabins. Each can comfortably accommodate 4 people; more if some are small children. The cabins have electric lighting, but no running water. They are each equipped with a wood-burning stove. The cabins serve as sleeping quarters, as well as general living areas for individual family units.

Bath House

Of the two buildings that have running water, the bath house is the only with flushable toilets. Built in the spot where the dilapidated home once stood, we chose to designate one small building for bathroom purposes. Tying this one structure in with the existing plumbing and septic tank made the most sense to us. The bath house is outfitted with 4 toilets, 2 showers, and 2 sinks.

Large Multi-Use Building

Our retreat is organized according to a sort of "summer camp" layout. Everyone gets to sleep in their own quarters, but just about everything else is a "common area". Accordingly, we needed to establish places for things like cooking, eating, meeting, and all manner of miscellaneous functions. Rather than putting up a dozen separate buildings for these things, we decided to go with one larger building that would fulfill several needs all at once. The main kitchen is used for cooking, as well as a workspace for processing game and preparing food for storage. The building has a large dining room full of tables and chairs, which also serves as our "town hall" where the entire community can gather for any purpose. There is also a small room which serves as the infirmary, in which our medical supplies and equipment are kept. A utility room is located near the back of the building, in which the batteries and other components of the off-grid electrical system are located. Besides for the bath house, this is the only building that has running water. This building is equipped with two wood-burning stoves, and is also outfitted with a conventional forced-air heating system that is fueled by a large propane tank on the property.

Storage Units

There are 3 small buildings that are used for storage and other purposes. The first is dedicated specifically to storing food preps. All types of dried/non-liquid food are stacked floor-to-ceiling in this unit. The second is used as a tool shed and workshop. Gardening equipment and tools are stored here, and it is also a workspace for repairing/building things. The third storage unit is considered "miscellaneous" storage, and is used for a variety of different things that need somewhere to go. The storage units are not heated, though the "workshop" unit does have electrical.

Security/Administration Office

A small building, approximately 300 square feet, that is used as an office. Important documents are kept here, along with our growing library of books and manuals. This building is also considered somewhat of a "security headquarters," as the radio base station is located here. Additionally, a reinforced and secured room serves as the retreat's "armory". The office is wired for electricity. It has a wood-burning stove, and a small heater that is fueled by propane.

In addition to the buildings, there are 4 other structures that have been constructed within the compound.

Greenhouse

Located in the "garden" area of the compound, a small greenhouse has been setup (technically the greenhouse is currently in-progress). This will expand our vegetable-growing capabilities, as seeds can be started earlier in the year. By the time the frost is over in the spring, young plants will have already sprouted and be ready for planting in the ground.

Chicken Coop

A coop that is big enough to accommodate up to 30 chickens has been built near the garden. An area around the coop has been sectioned off with chicken wire to keep the birds contained (and away from the garden!).

Outhouses

Because redundancy is key and everything needs a backup plan, there are 2 rustic outhouses located near the bath house.

Systems/Infrastructure

Electrical

Because the dining hall/kitchen has the largest surface area of any structure in the camp, the roof of this building is adorned with several solar panels. There are also 4 small wind turbines affixed to vertical pole mounts that are located on this building. All of the panels and turbines are wired in to a charge controller located in this building's utility room. The charge controller feeds into a bank of deep-cycle 12 volt batteries, which in turn are connected to a power inverter system. From the inverter, wiring is run out to the various spots within the retreat that need off-grid electricity. Since we already had an industrial-strength trenching tool on hand for burying some of the plumbing, we went ahead and buried the electrical wiring as well. Without a series of overhead wires, there is a much lower chance of damage or catastrophic failure of the electrical system due to wind, falling branches, etc.

While certain buildings on the property are connected to municipal electrical services, our solar/wind system is an entirely separate "grid". It's true that we could have tied the systems in together and saved some time and resources, but we considered it worthwhile for them to be entirely independent systems. No matter what happens with the municipal grid, it cannot affect our backup system. Power surges, power drains, or any other electrical hazard will not be able to cause damage to our backup system's components.

Plumbing

The two places in the retreat that have running water are the bath house and kitchen. These are also the only two places that are tied in to the septic system. While it would be awesome to have running water, showers, and toilets in every structure, we agreed that it would be more reasonable to only have these facilities in the places they were absolutely needed. Since the property was already supplied with a well and a septic tank, it was a matter of running some new pipes to the bath house and kitchen, and installing the new fixtures in both places. As long as the electrical system is functional and the batteries are charged, the pump will provide water straight from the well to the faucets. And, of course, let's not forget the hand well pump in case the electric pump isn't working for some reason.

Radio Communications

Our radio setup is probably more elaborate than it needs to be. One of our members is a serious amateur radio enthusiast, and he sort of took the ball and ran with it. I'm certainly not complaining! Our camp is equipped with a Ham base station, and enough handheld radios to supply every adult in the group. The handheld radios are capable of transmitting on

Ham bands, as well as MURS, FRS, and GMRS channels. While only three of us are licensed Ham operators, this will not be a legal concern during an emergency situation. Also located in the "security office" is a CB radio, though its purpose is primarily for monitoring the CB channels in case there is anyone nearby communicating on them. A vertical pole is attached to the security/office building, and extends above the roofline to 24 feet from the ground. Attached to this pole is the Ham antenna, as well as a separate CB antenna.

Perimeter

The area within our compound is about 3 acres. It is not a perfect square, or even a rectangle. It is closer to the shape of a trapezoid, with sides that taper in towards the driveway. At this time, the perimeter is delimited by what looks to the naked eye like a basic wooden privacy fence. In the efforts of keeping the place looking like some sort of hunting camp or vacation property to any miscellaneous passersby, we decided to forego a more aggressive-looking border wall.

To build a fence or wall around 3 acres of irregularly-shaped property, we would need approximately 1500 linear feet worth of materials. Even with the most modest of fence, this comes out to a lot of work and a lot of expense. While the thought of a 20 foot high medieval curtain wall makes my mouth drool, I don't happen to have a million bucks lying around to spend on a hundred tons of masonry, a fleet of dump trucks, and an army of old-timey stoneworkers. So my group had to come up with a solution that would be somewhere within the realm of reason, but still be able to serve as an effective fortification barrier.

A common wooden privacy fence is built with 4x4 posts, spaced 8 feet apart, and anchored into the ground with cement. Our fence follows the same concept, except we used 4x6 timbers for the posts, and spaced them only 6 feet apart. Using 12 foot timbers, 4 feet are buried in concrete underground. This gives us an above-ground height of 8 feet. Rather than digging about 250 individual post holes, we dug a single trench along the entire perimeter. The posts were then placed and supported with braces in their assigned spots. Finally, the entire trench was filled in with cement, with just enough space leftover for a thick layer of dirt. Digging a single trench ended up being easier than hundreds of individuals holes, and having a subterranean wall of cement helps ensure that no pesky animal (or person) is going to be tunneling under the fence anytime soon. While close to completion, this fence has been a work in progress for a couple of years. As time and resources are available, another phase or section gets built. First it was digging the trench. Then setting the posts and pouring concrete. Next, stringer boards were attached between the posts. Slowly but surely, the vertical pickets are getting installed. This requires a lot of pickets, and a lot of time. Ultimately, two gates will be installed. One wide gate at the main entrance to the compound that is wide enough for vehicles and machinery, and another narrow gate that can be used as a "backdoor" should we need to make an exit through the property's rear.

Finally, the surrounding woods help to facilitate yet another layer of protection. While not exactly considered part of the perimeter itself, the forest outside of the camp is invaluable in keeping people, animals, and vehicles away. The trees surrounding our perimeter are used to support large heaps of brush, sticks, branches, logs, and whatever other natural materials we have cleared from within the compound. This creates a berm, of sorts, that is very difficult to climb through. It would take awhile to maneuver through the heap, and it would take even longer to try and clear a section of it to make way for people or vehicles.

Infrastructure/Utilities

If your operational plan calls for your retreat to have electricity, running water, or any other utility or sanitation systems, you are going to have to consider the infrastructure that will be required to make it happen. If you are content to bail fresh water out of the nearby creek, and venture off into the woods every time nature calls, then maybe this section doesn't apply. If you have no intentions of having even the most basic of electrical capabilities, then infrastructure might not be among your concerns. But if the goal is to survive and thrive for months or years, I bet I'm not the only one who places a good deal of importance on the convenience and capabilities that some simple utilities can offer.

Electrical

While the fundamental systems in my group's retreat do not rely solely on electricity, we determined that it would be worth the investment to have certain capabilities that are made possible by having it. With a basic system of solar panels and small wind turbines, we can charge a bank of batteries which then provide the power needed to run a handful of things.

Our objectives for electrical power are pretty narrow in scope. Here is a short list of what our simple system will power if the municipal power grid is down:

- Lights - Modern LED light bulbs don't use a lot of juice, so it was a no-brainer to outfit each building with a little bit of electric lighting. It's just so much easier and safer than oil lamps or candelabras!

- Water pump - All it takes is a water source, an electric pump, and some pipes to have running water. We considered it a priority to have a fresh water supply to the kitchen and washroom. This was a major selling-point for my group when it came to the topic of electric power.

- Radios - For operations and security purposes, we agreed that radio communication is an important component for our retreat. Accordingly, we need electricity to power the base station and to charge the mobile radios.

Our small grid was designed to power these three key features at a bare minimum. On an average day, it has the capacity to power a bit more than this, so we have some various electrical devices and appliances that may get used. It's nice to have a fan on a hot day, and having a television and AM/FM radio would be pretty handy for monitoring the state of things (should such transmissions still be getting made).

I'm a realist. I understand that the useful lifespan of a battery will eventually come to an end. I know that solar panels and the components of a turbine also have an expected shelf life. But I've said before that I believe most realistic scenarios involving a catastrophic breakdown of society and the supply chain will not last more than a couple years. If I'm right, then we'll have more juice than we can use! If I'm wrong, the jig will eventually be up and our electrical capabilities will ultimately dwindle away. Luckily we have planned for that possibility, and our stock of oil lamps and candles is proof!

If your group decides that having electrical power is a necessity (or even just a luxury you don't want to live without), try to figure out anything and everything you may want to do with that power. From utility purposes, to entertainment, consider every appliance and device that might need juice. Make a list of the "must have" and the "could do without". I can't recommend solar and wind enough, as it is entirely renewable.

Plumbing

There is nothing quite as luxurious as running water. Every citizen of a developed nation in the modern era surely takes this simple utility for granted every single day, but it truly is a marvelous amenity to have. By the pure relativity of things, we aren't really capable of realizing how valuable it is unless we are in a situation where we don't have it. If you have the means to do so, I highly recommend establishing even a basic plumbing system for your retreat.

A water source, a pump, and some pipes are the main ingredients for a running water system. For a wastewater system, a septic tank and field are the common ways to go. If your retreat is anything like mine, it will be utilized during non-emergency situations. My group spends time at the retreat during all parts of the year. Until the compound is needed to serve as a survival retreat, it's really just a couple of cabins and some outbuildings that people use. It's a no-brainer that we would want running water and septic, regardless if society has collapsed.

In most cases, the water source will be a well. But if you have a body of water nearby, that can work too. A stream or lake can easily serve as your camp's fresh water source, but you have to consider issues with freezing during any cold months.

As mentioned in the previous section, having a fresh water supply will require a pump. For the couple of buildings at my retreat that have running water, an electric pump has to be used. This is one of the primary uses of our solar and wind electrical setup. However, a hand-pump is installed outdoors so that we can still access water from the well should the electric pump ever fail or the juice stops flowing for any reason. If an off-grid electrical system is outside of your group's capabilities or budget, you can still have plenty of fresh water with a manual pump and some elbow grease.

Septic

People got by just fine for hundreds of years with a good old-fashioned outhouse. A hole dug in the ground with a simple shack over top did the job it needed to do. A rustic outhouse is an entirely viable option for the bathroom needs of your group. But as I've said, your retreat may very well serve as a place of lodging during times other than the "apocalypse". Unless circumstances call for your retreat to be "activated," it's really just a remote place that people visit. So I say, "Why *wouldn't* you have a functional and comfortable bathroom?"

If you've already got running water, consider burying a septic tank. Of course this relies on having the resources, the time, and the physical room to do it. Having a sanitary way to handle this most basic human need should be considered a priority, whether it's a trusty outhouse or a flushing toilet. Believe me when I say that "where to go number two" is going to be the last thing you want to worry about while struggling to stay alive and safe.

Radio

This one may be considered more of a luxury to some, but my group agreed that it's as much a "must have" as it is a "want to have". The ability to immediately and accurately communicate with other members of the group can mean the difference between life and death. From assessing and combating an outside threat, to hunting animals for food, radio communications are a game-changer. In the old days, pretty much the only way to communicate over a distance was to send a runner. A person had to physically travel between parties in order to deliver a message. In a scenario without cell phones, instant messaging, landlines, computers, fax machines, or even the postal service, your options are pretty limited when it comes to relaying information to somebody who is not standing next to you.

While it should probably not be the first thing on your list, setting up some means of radio communication should be considered by your group. Depending on your budget, the distance you need to cover, and your group's communication objectives, there are a few options to choose from:

Amateur Radio (Ham)
While you must be licensed by the FCC to transmit on any amateur radio frequencies in normal circumstances, this does not apply during an emergency situation. Nevertheless, I would highly recommend that at least one person in your group becomes trained and licensed. The knowledge gained about radio communications alone is worth the trouble, not to mention being able to practice using Ham radio in the meantime.

A major benefit of Ham radio is that you can transmit and receive signals over great distances. Depending on your equipment, your proficiency, and atmospheric conditions, you could have a conversation with someone on the other side of the world!

Ham is the most versatile, powerful, and utilitarian option out there for radio communications. It's also among the most expensive and complicated options out there. Relying on amateur radio is probably going to be next to impossible without one or more people who are very knowledgeable and technically proficient when it comes to radio communications.

FRS/GMRS/MURS

The FCC has set aside certain radio frequencies for "general use" by the population. Used for somewhat short-range communications, these bands are commonly accessed by walkie-talkie style radios. Good for distances of only a few miles (or less, depending on your terrain), radios that use the FRS, GMRS, or MURS bands are very popular among families and regular folks. The radios are very simple to use, and can work quite well over short distances. But they are pretty limited in versatility, and are not very powerful. Federal law places a relatively low transmitting power limit on these types of radios, due to their intended purpose of close-range use by untrained civilians.

FRS - Family Radio Service. Commonly used with walkie-talkie style radios, FRS is used for short-distance communications by individuals. No license is required to use a FRS radio, though they are limited to transmit at no higher than 0.5 watts. These are the most common type of consumer-grade walkie-talkies and are regularly sold in retail stores of all types.

GMRS - General Mobile Radio Service. Designed for short-distance communications, GMRS frequencies require a license in the United States. There is no training or testing required for the license, but you must pay a small fee to the FCC to receive a license that is valid for five years. An adult can purchase a license, and the license is valid for that adult and any immediate family members. A typical GMRS radio transmits at between 1 and 5 watts, but can legally transmit up to 50 watts. GMRS radios are allowed to have detachable/external antennas.

MURS - Multi-Use Radio Service. An unlicensed two-way service, MURS frequencies can be used by the general public for personal or business purposes. MURS-approved radio equipment is limited at 2 watts for transmitting.

CB Radio

Short for "Citizen Bands," CB radio falls under a selection of forty channels within the 11 meter band. Popular with truckers and enthusiasts, CB has been around for decades. While capable of transmitting over greater distances than other "general use" bands, CB is still considered a short-range communication system. Depending on your equipment and antennas, CB can work very well for communicating over several miles. Like FRS, GMRS, and MURS, there are a relatively small number of available channels/frequencies available for CB. This means that the chances of other people listening or transmitting on the same channel as you are much higher than with Ham radio.

Commercial Radio System
Using technology similar to the other two-way radio systems, commercial radio systems are utilized by companies of all shapes and sizes to stay in touch for the purposes of normal business operation. Golf courses, ship yards, and warehouses, for example, equip employees with walkie-talkies in order to stay in constant communication with one another, as well as fixed base stations.

Any commercial entity that utilizes a radio communications system must be licensed by the FCC, and operate within the assigned business-band frequencies and laws that are specific to commercial operation. While there are many options available for commercial radio systems, I don't personally recommend this route because you will be unable to use it without expensive licensing. This won't be too much of a concern if there is no rule of law, but in the meantime you will not be legally able to use all of that expensive equipment you purchased.

The reason I am including radio communications in this section about infrastructure is that, depending on how you go about it, it may require some substantial considerations. An effective system often involves a base station and several mobile units. The base station would be located at the retreat, as it has a larger (and more powerful) transceiver and a tall antenna. Because it requires more electricity and a larger antenna, the base station is generally something that stays setup in one place. Between powering the base station and charging the batteries for the mobile radios, having radio communications pretty much requires having an electrical system. In my group, we consider the large Ham antenna itself to be a component of infrastructure.

The topic of radio communications is a vast and fascinating one, and you owe it to yourself to explore it much more deeply. There are many great books and websites about amateur radio and radio communications in general, so there's not one single resource that I can recommend for learning more. I would encourage anyone who is interested in this subject to get started by learning the basics of amateur radio. Or take it a step further and work towards getting your amateur radio technician license! If you're interested, get started at www.arrl.org, the official website for the *National Association for Amateur Radio*.

Preparing and Supplying Your Retreat

Acquiring land and setting up the basic shelters and infrastructure are undoubtedly the most daunting parts of setting up a survival retreat. It involves a level of commitment and expense that most people are not willing or able to devote. But the preparedness-minded folks who are in it for the long-haul understand the importance of sustaining quality of life in a system that can quickly fall apart. So for the select few who have committed to establishing a long-term bug-out compound, the work is far from over once construction is finished.

Once you have your location, your buildings, your infrastructure, and perimeter figured out, it's time to prep. Ideally, a survival retreat should strive to be a fully self-sufficient homestead as quickly as possible. But if it's not being run in such a way *until* there is reason to do so, your group will obviously have to live off of stored supplies in the meantime. How long that time period is likely to be must be figured out by your group during the planning phase. Early on, my group decided that we want to be able to run entirely off prepped food and supplies for a period of no less than five years, if absolutely necessary. If we have successful gardens, bountiful hunts, and a healthy flock of chickens, of course we will utilize those food resources in the meantime. But absent all other sources of nutrition, we agreed to stock our retreat with a minimum of five years' worth of food and supplies.

I'm sure it doesn't take a mathematician to know that feeding and supplying 20+ people for five years involves assembling an awfully big prep. It's why we have an entire storage building dedicated specifically to keeping dry foods!

Most people never think about the sheer quantity of food they consume in a year's time. But piling that much food together in one place really puts things into perspective.

As with prepping on any scale, you have to consider the following when planning a food store:

- Nutritional requirements of the average person, as well as the specific people in your group
- Foods with the longest shelf-life when properly stored
- Foods that you'll still want to eat after months or years
- Foods that you have the physical capabilities to prepare

What other things does the average person need throughout the course of a year? How about for children or pets? It's difficult to really visualize how much routine "stuff" we go through. How and where will you store months' or years' of toilet paper, soap, toothpaste, diapers, feminine products, and other personal hygiene items? How about clothes? I can wear through a few t-shirts and plenty of socks in a year's time. Ordinary, every-day items are often overlooked. As an exercise, make a very detailed list of every single non-food item that you consume in an average week. I think you will be surprised how much stuff you go through.

There are countless supplies, materials, and tools that a comprehensive retreat could have. The list will probably never stop growing. What supplies will you need for first aid, gardening, and food prep/cooking? What about recreation? Will you stock up on board games, playing cards, Frisbees, etc? Can you stock common spare parts for your equipment and systems? How about ammunition for all firearms? These are just a few ideas. A realistic list is bound to have hundreds or thousands of items on it.

Summary

Establishing and supplying your retreat is an incredible undertaking that can easily become an ongoing project that spans years or more. Every group must determine their own capacities and resources for establishing their survival compound. As part of your operational plan, you must consider what sort of facilities, infrastructure, and supplies will comprise your compound.

Whether it's simple or expansive, what sort of structures and/or buildings will you need?

- Sleeping/living quarters
- Kitchen/dining area
- Storage for food, supplies, and equipment.
- Bathroom or other wash facility
- Common area/gathering place
- Safe room/armory
- Shelter for livestock

Based on your group's needs and desires, what will your infrastructure include?

- Electrical
- Running water
- Septic system
- Communications
- Security, including perimeter

What will you need to prep for long-term storage, given your group's objectives?

- Food
- Water
- Toiletries
- Medical supplies
- Recreation
- Ammunition

Chapter 6
Bugging Out

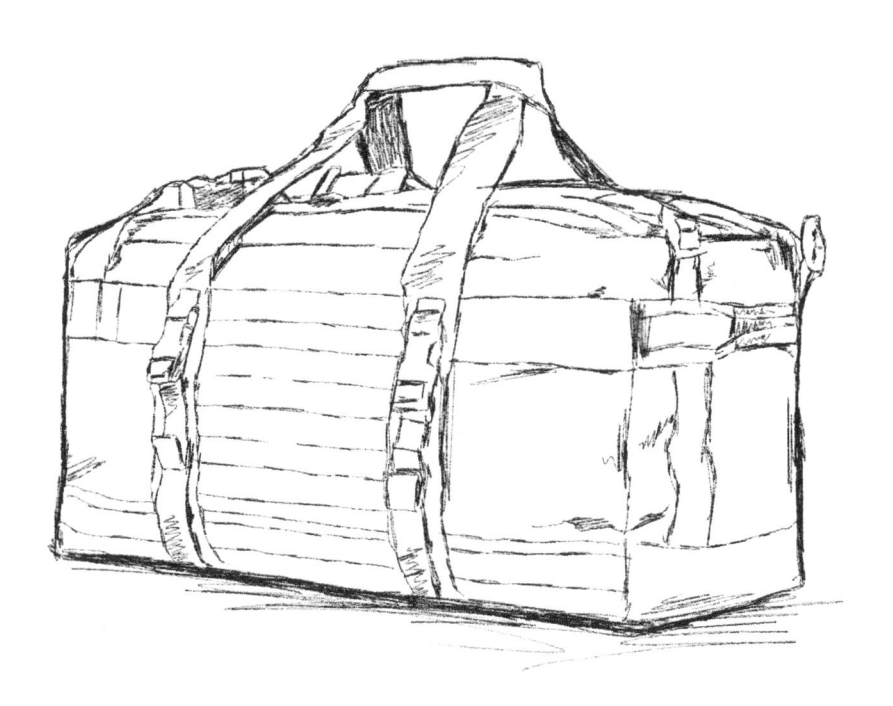

There is no one-size-fits-all plan for the bug-out procedure. This will ultimately be up to each individual or family to determine their best options for a bug-out plan. Some members may live closer to the retreat than others. Some may live close to each other, or scattered around a wider geographical area.

In my group, none of us live immediately near one another, so all bug-out protocol is on an individual basis. It's up to each of us to do what it takes to get to the retreat if SHTF. Since we're so spread out, we won't be of any help to one another until we are all together at the rendezvous point. If your group is spread out, each of you should have your own plan for getting out of town. If members live near one another, a joint plan could make sense. If possible, get each member's bug-out plan on paper and add it to the master operational plan. Having it in writing helps us stay on-point and aligned towards our objectives. It also serves as an action plan to follow if disarray and panic set in. The plans should be reviewed, practiced, and improved upon as necessary. I would encourage the group to meet and discuss each member's bug-out plan and offer insights to one another. As always, more brains are better!

Deciding When It's Time to Bug-Out

An aspect of the "bug out" that should be discussed at length is how you will all individually determine if/when the time has come to "get out of Dodge." It's impossible to know what the conditions will be in the early stages of society's fall. You may have cellular and other means of communications all throughout, even up to the time when the "call" is made. It's also very possible that no electronic communications can be relied upon when it gets to the point where a bug-out is necessary.

As a group, you have to decide what indicators will dictate when it is time to go. Civil unrest and natural disasters don't spring up overnight. We see them coming, at least somewhat, in advance. Something like a catastrophic electric grid failure won't likely come with any warning, which makes things trickier. As a group, you must figure out either:

- A way to stay in communication even if there is no cellular communication or electrical grid.
- An event or some sort of indication to signal everybody when it is time to initiate the bug-out plans.

If you are able to communicate within the group, it can be as simple as a code phrase. Heck, you could just say "Time to go," and make sure the message reaches all members of the group. If communication isn't possible between all members, you will have to decide what you will collectively consider to be "the last straw." Here are a few examples of what you could consider as the "indicator" for initiating bug-out protocol:

- The electrical grid for an entire region (or worse) has gone down, and the power has been out for 14 days. On day 15, you all know to bug-out.
- A certain level of civil unrest or lawlessness has been observed. This one may be more difficult to define. If one member begins to witness acts of lawlessness in the streets where he or she lives, that does not necessarily mean that all of the other members are witnessing similar things taking place yet.
- Absence of other utilities or municipal services. Whether or not the power grid goes down, other utilizes could begin to fail. Your city water, internet, or phone lines could stop flowing due to an act of sabotage or terrorism, or simply because utility workers are no longer doing their jobs. If things have gotten to the point where essential personnel have abandoned their posts, you probably should have already bugged-out by then.
- News of invasion, attack, outbreak, etc. Even without mass communication, word would spread pretty quickly if something as significant as a foreign attack or invasion is taking place. It probably goes without saying that such news should be considered your bug-out indicator.

It's important that all members of the group are in congruence regarding *when* to bug out. The entire point of your survival community relies on everybody being there. Individually you are weak; together you are strong.

A wise man once said, "Shit happens." Of course it is possible that not everybody will arrive at the rendezvous point at the exact same time. They almost certainly won't. There are many variables which can majorly affect travel times even when society is purring along just fine, let alone when everything is going to Hell! Even if all members head out at the exact same time, there is no telling how many variable factors could cause problems and delays. Add to that the fact that all members won't live the exact same distance away from the rendezvous, it's probably impossible for every member of the group to be so coordinated that everyone arrives at precisely the same time. Nevertheless, it's important that everybody arrive in as close a proximity as possible. I would aim for the same day. This should be taken into consideration as each member assembles their individual bug-out plan. Each member should do what it takes to arrive at the rendezvous at some point during the same day.

Closing Up Shop

I'm not going to spend a lot of time on this point, as this is more of an operational phase that should be considered and executed on an individual level. If the time comes where you must bug out, you should have some thoughts in place for what to do with the place *from* which you are bugging. For most of us this means our home. You are about to leave your home, and you have no idea for how long. You may return in a few days, or never. There may be no way of predicting which it will be.

If you will be gone for an indefinite amount of time, you should probably accept the idea that your home may be pillaged, plundered, or worse. Nevertheless, on the chance that it is left unscathed by the unprepared hordes, you may want to ensure its habitability should you be able to return. This may involve shutting of the water supply and opening your faucets so pipes don't freeze. It may mean shutting down your furnace or turning off all your circuit breakers. I recommend burying or taking any irreplaceable items, such as family heirlooms or documents.

You might also consider leaving a (coded) message in the house, should any family members come looking for you. It's up to each person to determine the state in which they leave their home. Of course, time may not permit anything more elaborate than grabbing your bug-out gear and disappearing. It's just another item to consider in the name of preparedness.

Transporting People and Supplies

As I've said, your group should have every possible aspect of your collective "bugging out" planned out as thoroughly as it can be planned. Since my group's retreat has full-time residents, it is more plausible for us to keep much of our supplies and food preps on-site since people are always there to act as stewards, groundskeepers, overseers, etc. But some groups will seek to transport much of their equipment and preps to the compound at the time of bug-out.

When transporting people and a bunch of stuff, you either need a big vehicle, multiple small vehicles, or possibly a vehicle plus a trailer. I'm a fan of the "big vehicle plus big trailer" method, because I can transport a few people and a lot of stuff all in one shot. I also have room for spare tires, spare gas cans, and spare everything-else-I-can-think-of.

However you plan to do it, whether you will be taking only your family and the clothes on your back or a ton of supplies, you should be hashing out all the logistics well before the time comes. A full-on trial run is a huge pain, but you have to do it! When your plan is in place and all your preps are ready, conduct a full-scale dry run. Load up the vehicle, trailer, etc. Have everyone in your household execute the bug-out plan down to the last detail. Practice taking your primary route and secondary route to the bug-out location.

As with everything, each group and individual's plan may vary when it comes to bug-out procedure. But the point that needs to be drilled into our heads is that we have to *have* that plan, and we have to practice executing that plan.

Rendezvous Point

In most cases, the "rendezvous point" will simply be your retreat. Everyone meets up at the retreat on the same day after bugging-out. However, there may be cases where it's necessary or preferred that the rendezvous point is another location. This is up to your group to discuss and decide. A couple reasons I can think of why a group may decide to use an alternate rendezvous point are:

- The retreat is in an incredibly remote location that is not accessible by all members' vehicles. In an ideal situation, everybody would have a heavy-duty, off-road capable vehicle. Of course, this isn't always realistic. If one or more of your members are driving small cars that will have no chance of getting down the dirt two-track leading to the retreat, you may need to meet at another location and head in from there. To take this a step further, it's possible that a group's retreat may actually be accessible only by water (such as a small island). Unless every member has their own boat at the ready, traveling to the island retreat would require meeting up and traveling in together on the available watercraft.

- There are security-related concerns about individual members being followed to the retreat by strangers. The last thing you want is for desperate outsiders to come upon your retreat when you aren't yet prepared to deal with it. It's worth considering the idea that nobody actually goes all the way to the retreat until *everybody* goes.

- There is a concern that outsiders could have found, and are currently at, the retreat. Again, this is not something that one or two individual members should attempt to deal with. Such a scenario is a very serious and potentially dangerous situation. If there is any worry that strangers are trying to set up shop in your survival compound, you should go in as a group, and go in with a plan.

Summary

Your survival retreat doesn't do your group any good if you aren't able to get there in a time of crisis. Once your bug-out location is ready to rock, you will need to refine your plans for how to get there quickly and safely.

- Establish a guideline for what the group considers bug-out "triggers". Everyone should know *when* to bug-out.
- Is there anything you need to do to close up your home before leaving to improve the chances that it will still be in good shape if/when you return? Consider any last-minute securing of the premises, as well as turning off the water, gas, and/or electricity.
- How will you transport all the people and supplies that need to make it

Prepper Community

to the bug-out location? Will everything fit in your vehicle? Will you use a trailer or secondary vehicle? Do you have a secondary route planned in case the main road is obstructed or inaccessible?

- If not the retreat itself, your group should establish a rendezvous point and estimated timeline of when each member will arrive.

Chapter 7
Retreat Activation

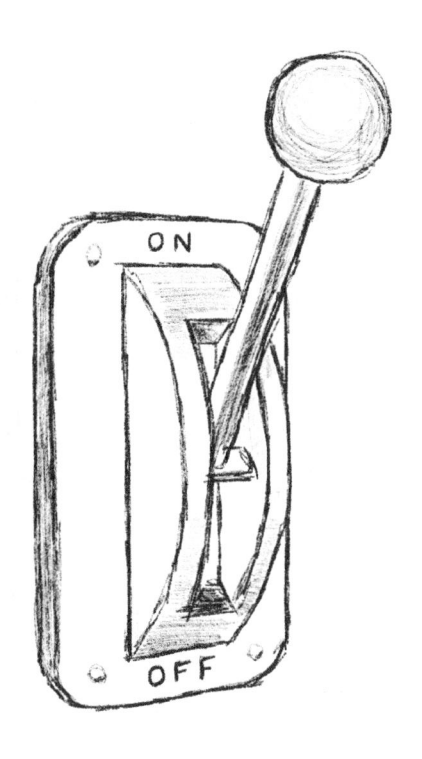

What does it mean to activate your retreat? It means "bring it to life". Fire up the systems and protocol for anything and everything, according to your operational plan. It means checking and securing the perimeter. It means making sure the water is accessible and ready to use. It means checking that all of your systems are functioning properly, and all of your members are aware of their immediate duties. If it's winter, it means firing up the wood-burning stoves. If you have any essential supplies buried, it means digging them up.

Activating your retreat is a combination of initiating your essential systems and battening down the hatches.

Security is Step One in the activation of your compound. Refer to your carefully-crafted operational plan for what that means. At my retreat, it means that nobody goes anywhere without their rifle and a buddy. It means vehicles are parked to block the gates and the couple of weaker points in the perimeter. It means round-the-clock patrolling of the grounds. It means checking the radios to make sure the batteries are good and everyone is in communication with everyone else at all times. Once the wagons are circled and the hatches are battened, you can begin the next phase according to your operational plan.

Short-Term Operation

In most realistic scenarios, order and services will be restored in a matter of days or weeks. As I mentioned previously, Americans are resilient and crave normalcy. This means that it's likely you will only have to operate your retreat for a short time before it's clear to return to your normal lives. For this reason, you should initially operate according to your "short-term" plan. This involves using your stored food and supplies. Until you have a very compelling reason to believe that this is going to be a much longer endeavor, stick to the short-term plan.

Long-Term Operation

For my group, the long-term plan addresses food and water as a priority. We can live on our stores for quite some time, but not forever. Supplementing the stored food with fresh meat and produce is a significant part of our long-term operational plan. Depending on the time of year, vegetables will get planted in the prepared garden spaces. Fishing and hunting parties will be sent out to nearby areas. We are currently working on adding a greenhouse to the retreat, so that vegetable gardening can be done during more months of the year.

A long-term plan will also come with increased security measures. The longer it's been since society has turned on itself, the greater the chances that people will happen across your group (and the greater the risk that they will commit desperate acts). There will likely be great exoduses from the cities a short while after collapse. More people going to less-populated areas increases the odds that someone will stumble upon your camp. If you are battening down for the long haul, you should constantly reinforce your security measures. This could include building blinds in trees to serve as watchtowers. It could include adding additional layers to the perimeter wall, such as stockade fencing or massive piles of scrub that will hinder movement from the outside.

Read more about retreat security in Chapter 14.

Once your long-term plan is fully initiated, your retreat should be running like a full-fledged homestead (albeit more protected than a traditional homestead). Food production and storage, water gathering and filtration, cooking, sanitation, firewood, and security should all be working in harmony. If your long-term plan is successful, all of the basic needs of your group's members should be fulfilled indefinitely.

Chapter 8
Leadership and Member Roles

There are many ways your membership can be organized. Some groups prefer something along the lines of a military format, with similar ranks and structure. Others go with an absolute democratic process in which there is no defined leadership and everything is voted on equally by all members. Some groups operate according to something resembling a corporate structure. Your group should decide what makes the most sense to you, and no one solution will be perfect for everyone. Keeping that in mind, I'll outline the basic organizational structure of my group for you to reference as an example.

The group to which I belong has three primary types of members in its

Thomas Eddy

organizational structure:

Senior Leadership

- Hierarchically speaking, all members of the senior leadership are considered equal. None outrank the others.
- In the case of my group, these members are known as the "founding members".
- Senior leaders are also considered voting members.
- Though equal from a leadership perspective, each senior member is responsible for a particular component of the community/retreat. In the event of a tied vote on a particular issue, the tie will be broken by the senior member whose specialty is most relevant to the issue at hand. Our senior leadership consists of five members, and the areas for which they are responsible include:
    - Security - Responsible for implementing security measures and overseeing security patrols.
    - Medical - Responsible for first aid and any other medical needs that may arise.
    - Agriculture - Responsible for food production, including vegetable crops and livestock.
    - Engineering - Responsible for mechanical and infrastructure demands, including construction, vehicle repair, and maintenance of existing systems.
    - Logistics/Operations - Responsible for community planning, coordinating resources , and managing the overall operation of the retreat. If a tied vote must be broken and does not obviously fall into any of the other four specialties, the senior leader responsible for logistics/operations will cast the deciding vote.

Voting Members

- All contributing members of the group are considered "voting members".
- Contributing members are adults who have consistently added value to the community since the time they joined. They have actively contributed time, knowledge, materials, and/or funds to the effort.
- Voting members have a say in all issues that come up for a vote.
- All voting members have a role in the community, and "report to" one of the five senior members.

Non-Voting Members

- Members who are not considered contributing members are non-voting members.
- In most cases, non-voting members are the spouses or children of contributing members.
- While they obviously belong to the community should the retreat ever be activated, these members have not contributed to the creation of the retreat and have not been actively involved in the community before SHTF.
- Non-voting members who are able-bodied and capable will have work roles and report to senior leadership like everybody else. However, they do not necessarily have a say in community issues that come up for a vote.
- Non-voting members can become voting members after SHTF if the current voting members are in agreement on the matter.

As I said, there are a million different ways you may choose to structure your group. The founding members of my group are businessmen more-so than soldiers or politicians, so we felt most comfortable with something resembling a corporate organizational structure. My aim in this chapter is to give you some ideas. The important thing is that these matters are discussed and agreed upon early in the planning phase. Leaving any of this up to interpretation will only invite chaos and disagreements down the road. You owe it to yourselves to nail down how you will handle leadership and member roles.

Thomas Eddy

Chapter 9
Food

Providing your group with precious calories is going to be a constant initiative. In an environment with no grocery stores and nobody to rely upon except yourselves, you will need to spend plenty of time and resources to ensure that everybody will eat.

Let's talk about the food sources that will likely be available after bugging out.

Stored Food

Every prepper worth his or her salt is going to have some amount of food preps stored for a rainy day. As a group, you must determine how much food to store based on your anticipated caloric needs and how long you want your supply to last. Keep in mind that your best bet will be to prep food for long-term storage. Unless you can cycle through a large quantity of stored food in quicker intervals, you should probably aim for food items that can store for 10 or more years. Many other resources already go into incredible detail about what kinds of food to store and the various ways of storing them, so I'm not going to elaborate much further on this. Just be sure to store enough food to cover your entire group for the duration of what you've determined to be your retreat's short-term operation.

Foraging

If you have the knowledge to do it safely, foraging for edible things in the wilderness can supplement your food plan. Depending on your location, you may be able to find various edible berries, nuts, roots, plants, and mushrooms. Additionally, herbal teas and medicinal concoctions can be made from a variety of ingredients that the forest has to offer. While I don't consider foraging to be a primary food source, it's a source nonetheless.

Gardening

Providing your own food is the absolute key factor to the long-term sustainability of your homestead. If you had to learn as much as possible about any one thing, organic vegetable gardening is what I would recommend. There's no measure to how valuable a diverse vegetable garden will be to your group, nor to the value of any person who is very knowledgeable about managing one. From composting to pest management, growing a successful garden without fancy store-bought fertilizers and sprays is a challenging endeavor and will require constant attention. The sustainability of your group depends on a healthy yield, so commit as many resources as necessary to the gardening efforts.

When creating your supply list, make sure to account for tools, twine, stakes, irrigation lines, and anything else you could possibly need to set up and maintain a large garden.

Raising Animals

Livestock is another no-brainer on any self-sufficient homestead. Humans have been raising animals as a food source since the early days of civilization. If you have the space, the resources, and the knowledge, you could raise all manner of livestock. For most groups, however, it's probably logistically unrealistic to plan on raising large animals like cows or sheep. That's why chickens and rabbits are so popular among homesteaders and preppers. Chickens taste great and provide calories and fats that we need. They produce eggs, eat bugs, and can cultivate new ground for your garden. In my opinion, chickens are a must-have. Rabbits are also popular to raise as a food source because they multiply frequently and they grow quickly. You can also consider keeping a goat or two, which can provide milk, butter, and cheese while not requiring nearly as much space or resources as a dairy cow.

Keep in mind what sorts of materials and equipment you may need throughout the process of raising animals for food. Feed troughs, water buckets, and shelter/cages will be needed for the animals. Also, what tools for slaughtering and butchering will be needed when the time comes? Lastly, how much of your gardening space will you have to commit to growing food for the animals?

Hunting and Trapping

Every "wannabe" survivalist and prepper likely has some notion that he or she will bug out to the middle of nowhere and then rely on the land to provide. But those who are actually hunters know that it's not quite so simple or easy. Hunting takes a lot of skill, patience, and luck. The same is true for trapping. You need the right equipment, the right knowledge, and the right opportunities. They are skills to learn and develop, because finding fresh meet in the wilderness in an invaluable resource if you can do it. A large game animal like deer, elk, or moose can feed a group of people. But small game like squirrels, rabbits, and birds are nothing to scoff at. A couple of squirrels can make a fine stew for dinner. If society and law have deteriorated, it's a survival situation and things like hunting seasons and licensing aren't going to come into play. Hunting and/or trapping should be a constant effort, particularly if you aren't getting meat from livestock.

Fishing

Similar to hunting and trapping, fishing is a no-brainer. If you are near a body of water that fish can be found in, you should be fishing! Use a net, a spring-loaded hook, or a natural fish trap and check it regularly. If you are lucky enough to be close to a source of fresh protein, be sure to take advantage of it.

Chapter 10

Water

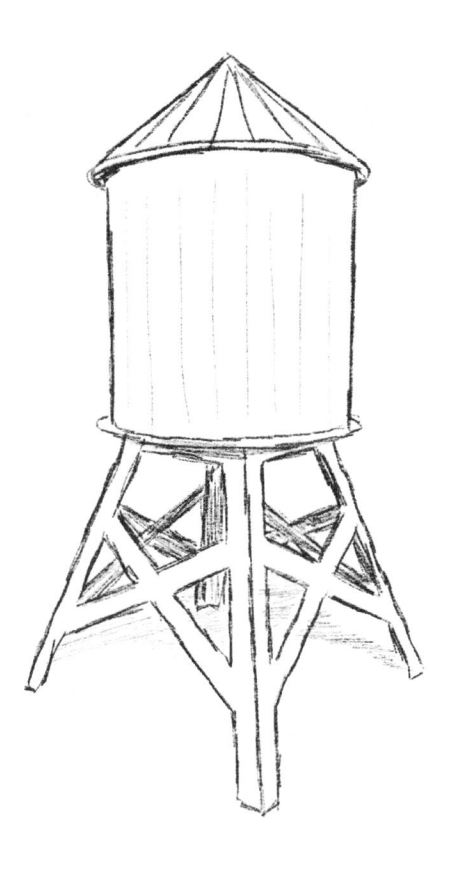

At a bare minimum, people require about 1 gallon of water per day for drinking, cooking, and sanitation purposes. If your group consists of 20 people, that works out to around 600 gallons of water per month. While it's a great idea to have some clean water stored for your retreat's short-term operation, it becomes logistically prohibitive to store enough water to last for several months or years.

Efforts should be made to constantly replenish your clean water reserves. This involves collecting water from a source, purifying it, and storing it.

Collecting Water

There are 3 natural sources that you will likely be able to tap for fresh water.

Rainwater

Collecting rainwater is an obvious way to passively accumulate fresh water. Ideally, every structure in your camp should be outfitted with gutters that feed into rain barrels. What's even better is if these rain barrels are set atop an elevated stand of some sort. This way the barrels can use gravity to feed irrigation lines to the garden.

Groundwater

Millions of households in the United States still use wells as their primary source of water. If you are able to dig a well and install a manual or electric pump, your camp can enjoy near-limitless fresh water on demand (depending on the water table, of course).

Bodies of Water

When all else fails, you can't go wrong with a bucket and a body of fresh water. A nearby lake, river, or stream would be able to provide your group with water probably forever. If your retreat is close enough, a system of hoses and pumps may even be possible so you don't have to lug those buckets every day.

Purifying Water

It should go without saying that any water meant for consumption or sanitation should be purified. While groundwater is filtered naturally, it should be further purified before use. Heavy metals, toxins, and parasites can be found in any natural water source. Water from stagnant, open bodies of water especially should be filtered and purified thoroughly before using for any purpose.

There are a few ways to purify your drinking water. Depending on the risk factors, you may implement more than one of these methods before considering your water "purified".

Boiling

Everybody is familiar with boiling water to sterilize it. There is basically no organism that can survive 5-10 minutes of full-on boiling. While it requires a lot of heat (and therefore fuel), there's no simpler method for killing bacteria and other creepy-crawlies. Keep in mind, however, that boiling does not remove all toxins. It kills organisms, but it *removes* nothing.

Filtration

Filtration is considered by many to be the most ideal of purification methods. It involves adding no chemicals to the water, it uses very little energy, and it removes almost all types of organisms and toxins. There are many types of water filters available, in every size and configuration imaginable. You can find very large gravity filters that are well-suited to a large quantity of water. This is what I recommend for your retreat. Perhaps the only downside to the filtration method is that the filtration elements eventually need to be replaced. Each filter is rated for a certain quantity of water before it is considered no longer effective. So if filtration is going to be your primary source of water purification, be sure to keep a stash of replacement filters on hand.

Distillation

Distillation is and incredibly effective way to purify water. Distillation involves boiling water, collecting the steam that is created, and then re-condensing that steam into water. While it requires a distiller (either home-made or store-bought) and lots of heat, distillation produces very pure water. I once watched a demonstration of distillation that involved pouring a bottle of black ink into the source water. At the end of the process, the distilled water was crystal clear. Everything that isn't water stays behind.

Chemical Treatment

Chemical additives have been used by backpackers and survivalists for a long time. Chemicals such as chlorine bleach and iodine are the most common disinfectant chemicals that are used for water purification. A few drops of bleach or iodine will kill nearly everything in a gallon of water. The downsides to these options are that bleach loses its potency after a few months in storage, and iodine makes water taste yucky. Chlorine dioxide is another additive that works very well to kill organisms in your water. Available in tablet form, chlorine dioxide doesn't make your water taste funny, and it has no expiration date.

UV Light

There are a variety of store-bought and home-made purification devices that utilize ultra-violet light to kill organisms in water. Considered one of the lesser effective methods of purifying water for drinking, UV light does not kill viruses or remove most toxins.

Storing Water

Once your water is collected and purified, all that's left to do is store it until use. On a large scale, such as in a community of 20-30 people, there are a couple different strategies for storing water.

One Big Container

Think of it like a city's water tower. One great big container to hold all of the camp's clean water reserves. There are a couple advantages to this method. You only need to haul water to one central place. If the water tank is elevated, you can rely on gravity to provide water pressure (and therefore running water) to the camp. On the other hand, this means that you will have to somehow get that water up to the elevated tank in the first place.

Large water tanks and cisterns come in many shapes, sizes, and materials. Depending on your climate, you may need a more durable material. You can also get large water tanks that are meant to be buried underground.

Many Smaller Containers

Picture 55 gallon water barrels everywhere you look, scattered inside and outside of each structure. If you don't have an elevated cistern and a means to deliver water around the camp, this may be the way to go. While it involves hauling water around to more locations, it also means that clean water is always quickly accessible to everybody. Another big advantage to having multiple smaller containers is in case of disaster. If one smaller container is punctured or leaks, there are still many others. However, if your lone 5,000 gallon cistern was to breach, you would have to pray that repairing it was a possibility. And in the meantime you would have 5,000 gallons of water flooding through camp!

However you choose to store water for your community, make sure to use containers that are appropriate for your climate and intended use. Keep them clean, and don't let them grow mildew, mold, or anything else that is going to get you sick.

Chapter 11

Heat

Simply put, we need heat to stay warm, to cook, and to clean. In the comfort of our homes right now, that tends to mean furnaces and appliances that run on natural gas, propane, or electricity. All three of these will be too scarce to rely upon for long-term heat at your compound. So how are you going to provide enough heat to keep everybody warm, cook food, and boil water?

If your retreat is located in an area that is even somewhat wooded, burning wood is the obvious answer. To the off-grid survivalist, wood is the ultimate renewable resource. While the answer is obvious, the execution is not necessarily easy. First, does your camp have multiple structures for living, or just one? If there are multiple structures, each one will need a heat source. How about a kitchen? You need a cooking appliance that burns wood.

Once you've determined how many wood-burning appliances you need, you'll have to decide which to use. A fireplace is one idea. While a fireplace can heat up a room, it's become more of a decorative feature in the modern age. Wood-burning stoves are generally considered more efficient, more safe, and more useful.

The Wood-Burning Stove

A wood stove is mostly enclosed. A hatch allows access for adding wood and cleaning, but it remains shut most of the time. This means that hot embers can't jump out, and smoke has only one place to go (out the smokestack).

They also burn more efficiently than a fireplace. You can get more heat with less wood. Fireplaces are usually enclosed on all sides but one by bricks. You can't access any heat from that fire except from one direction. A wood-burning stove is free-standing, and radiates heat from all sides.

Lastly, a wood-burning stove can also be used as a cooking appliance. Many styles of wood stove have flat tops, or even designated "burners" for placing pots and pans.

In short, it probably goes without saying that a wood-burning stove is a must-have for any structure you need to heat up. If you live in a warm climate and only need heat for cooking and boiling, a simple fire-pit will probably suit you just fine.

Storing Firewood

One way or another, you're going to be burning wood. Gathering that wood takes a lot of effort, but in the colder months it has to be done constantly. It should be a continuous effort to accumulate firewood. If the weather gets too cold, it may not be very easy to get out there to gather and chop wood. You'll want to have a sizable cache of firewood.

Choose carefully where you store your wood. You may decide to have a wood pile outside each structure, or in one central location. Wherever you choose, don't pile your wood directly against a structure (other than one designated solely for wood storage). Consider the insects and other pests that will take up residence in those wood piles. Keeping them at least a short distance away will make a huge difference in whether or not those critters will spread into your living quarters.

Another idea that some employ is to line up their stored firewood in long rows, almost like a fence. While only a few feet tall, that "wall" can serve a strategical purpose in addition to being an awesome cache of firewood. It can act as another layer in your security perimeter. It can help divert pooling water during heavy rains. It could possibly even work as a temporary corral for animals.

Chapter 12

Power

If your group decides that electrical power is a necessity at your camp, you will have to decide how you want to generate it. No matter how you accomplish it, generating power means consuming resources. Whether it's petroleum, wood, batteries, or elbow grease, you will have to spend resources to make power. Here are the most feasible options for supplying off-grid electricity for your group:

Gasoline/Propane

Conventional generators that run on gasoline or propane are widely available and affordable. While running, they are reliable and can output plenty of wattage. The obvious downside to a generator that consumes liquid fuel is that you will eventually run out of that fuel. You should also consider the maintenance that is required to keep an internal combustion engine operating properly.

Solar

It's clean, it's renewable, and it's relatively affordable. Solar power systems are more popular than ever. They come in every shape, size, and output. Systems can be entirely portable and compact, or scalable to any capacity you need. You'll need to invest in panels, batteries, and a charge controller. Once you're set up, you've got power for years (as long as you have enough batteries to store that power for nighttime and especially-overcast days).

Wind

Like solar, wind power systems come in every shape, configuration, and price range. Operating very similarly to a solar power system, a wind turbine generates electricity that gets stored in one or more large batteries. Additionally, it's pretty simple to use smaller wind turbines to subsidize a solar power setup. Panels and turbines work great together to charge those batteries.

Water

If you're lucky enough to have a flowing stream or river running through your camp, you could set up a water-powered turbine. Like solar and wind, this generated power is then stored in a battery bank until use.

Wood-Burning

There are some generators which use burning wood and steam to move a turbine and generate electricity. Such machines are pretty rare to find, and the couple that I have seen were home-engineered contraptions for the most part. There are also systems called wood gas generators that use gasification to convert wood and/or charcoal into combustible gases that power the generator. These would be great options to have on hand, but their availability and affordability make them less attractive than other power-generating options.

Human Power

You always have the option of going full Gilligan's Island! Plenty of people on YouTube have modified an exercise bike or manual treadmill to generate electricity when operated. It's not the way my group has chosen, but it's an option (or at least an interesting backup option).

Chapter 13

Sanitation

In an off-grid survival situation, effective sanitation and hygiene will be more important than ever. In our modern homes, it takes very little thought and very little effort to use the toilet and wash our hands. Everything is convenient and unlimited. But living in a place where basic hygiene isn't convenient or simple is no excuse to neglect it.

As educated, modern humans, we know that bacteria cause sickness. We know that disease spreads through dirty water and sewage. That's why we go to great lengths to keep our drinking water separate from our wastewater.

Thomas Eddy

That's why we wash our hands, and disinfect our bathrooms. That's why you must do the same when living post-SHTF. If you do get sick, access to medical care will likely be nonexistent.

Even if you have no formal bathroom or outhouse, you can keep it clean. Make sure to do your "business" away from the camp, and bury it. Dig a trench in advance, and use a small bit of that trench each time. Bury the part you used, and work your way down the line. When the trench is filled, dig a new one.

If you do have a bathroom or outhouse, take care to clean it like you would your bathroom at home. Make sure to wash your hands as regularly as you do right now. Try not to neglect bathing. Hot showers might not be as readily available, but a wash cloth and a bucket of warm water is easy enough.

What will you do about toilet paper? I stock rolls of toilet paper and keep them stored in wide PVC pipes with closed ends to keep out moisture and bugs. Most of us don't like to think about what we'll do when the TP runs out, but you have to. While not especially common in the United States, many people make use of a bidet or similar water-spraying device. While some argue that it's generally healthier than using dry toilet paper, the advantage in the scenarios we're preparing for are more about supply. There may be no supply of toilet paper, but if you have water and a means to spray it, you could be in good shape. Whether you decide to stock years' worth of toilet paper or go with a different solution, it's something you need to figure out.

The same applies with feminine hygiene products. What did humans use before modern disposable products were invented? Again, I'll leave that up to you to figure out. But you'd better figure it out!

Think about how you will wash your clothes. My group's tentative plan is to have a weekly community laundry day. We have one enormous wash tub, a manual clothes wringer, and plenty of clothesline. In the winter, the clothesline will hang indoors. Cleanliness is important for health and morale, so be sure to spend the time to plan out how you will manage it.

The last point I want to make on the topic of cleanliness is about food prep.

Prepper Community

Cross-contamination of raw meats will make you sick faster than anything. Nobody wants food poisoning in the best of circumstances. Whoever is in charge of butchery, food storage, food preparation, and/or cooking must be 100% diligent. When it comes to food handling, there's no room for error. Don't let anything touch any surface that has been touched by raw meat unless it's been cleaned first. Wash your surfaces. Wash your utensils. And most importantly, wash your hands!

Chapter 14
Retreat Security

Securing and protecting yourself after SHTF is perhaps the focus of more books, videos, and discussions than any other aspect of prepping/survivalist scenarios. We all know what desperate people are capable of, and we all know what people are willing to do when there is no fear of law or consequence.

Managing your retreat's security is no small undertaking. It can quite literally be the difference between life and death. And not every hypothetical scenario involves a band of soul-less marauders storming your camp. If somebody comes across a well-stocked compound, it would be far less risky for them to simply steal. So you shouldn't just be stockpiling artillery to ward off the bands of cut-throats. You need to batten down every corner of your retreat to keep out those who don't belong.

They say good fences make good neighbors. This will never be more true than if society crumbles and it's every man for himself. Keeping strangers out of your camp may be the difference between a disappointed stranger and a dead body.

I cannot possibly cover in a single chapter everything that needs to be covered about your retreat security. There are far better resources on the intricacies of securing, patrolling, and booby-trapping your compound.

See additional resources about retreat security in Chapter 18.

Multi-Layered Security Plan

The key is to a secure compound is to have a multi-layered plan that accounts for every foreseeable situation. In the absence of unlimited funds, it will be difficult to create a fully-automated system of remote sensors, laser-guided sentry guns, and roving kill-bots. So you'll likely be relying on more archaic security measures, such as walls, mechanical traps, and good old-fashioned human patrols.

As I said, this is a topic that deserves a much deeper drive than this book can provide. That being said, here are the basic facets of my group's security plan.

Stay Hidden

We're off the beaten path. The compound is surrounded by trees. Unless smoke or sound give us away, nobody is likely to find us except by sheer luck. Everybody wears some type of camo, so it's difficult for somebody at a distance to make out how many of us there are. We also make it a habit to create the least amount of noise possible. If we don't need to shout, we don't.

If we don't need to use a power tool, we won't. If we don't need to fire a gun, we don't.

Keep Strangers from Getting Close

Before a thief or cut-throat even gets to the point where they must contend with the security wall and patrol, they will have to deal with a series of obstacles, traps, and alerts. All around our perimeter wall we have piles of thorny, prickly scrub that would be quite difficult to sneak through.

In a SHTF scenario, we will install various traps and alerts in pre-designated spots in the woods leading up to the compound. Meant to injure, slow, and/or deter a trespasser, booby traps are an essential layer to our security plan. The alerts are meant to signal the camp that somebody is near, and provide an indication of the direction from which the threat is coming.

Keep Strangers Out

This is where the perimeter comes in. Making it very difficult for somebody to sneak or force their way in is a vital layer of any security plan. It's all about keeping them away from the group's supplies, the group's food, the group's firearms, the group's living quarters, and the group itself. During the night, there are always no fewer than two people patrolling the perimeter. Upon activating the retreat, large logs will be arranged across the only road access point, to keep any wayward vehicles out, and to prevent our gate from being rammed.

If Strangers Get In, Contain Them

This goes for human and animal strangers alike. I'm pretty sure I would react similarly to a hungry bear busting through my wall as I would a hungry human. Either way, they have to be contained before they can cause injury or damage. In a world with no law, this may very well mean using deadly force. But if somebody is trying to physically breach the sanctity of your home in order to take food out of the mouths of you and your group (or do something much worse), they have already assessed and made peace with the risks involved.

Weapons

Everybody has their own opinions on the topic of weapons. I think it's safe to assume that most Americans who identify as preppers or survivalists are probably pro-firearm to some degree. Either way, the reality is that desperate and evil people will seek to do desperate and evil things if our delicate system of law and order is not fully intact. That means you owe it to yourself to be prepared in the most effective ways possible to remain safe and alive. This means owning and carrying a firearm.

Great debates will always be had about what the "best" types of firearms are. Even more spirited debates are had about what caliber, brand, or model is the best gun to have post-SHTF. The specifics of which exact guns to arm yourself with is not for this book to determine or argue. As I've said, the aim of this book is to give you an idea of the many things your group will have to plan for. In the context security for your retreat, I advise that you plan for every able-bodied adult to be armed at all times.

My group's security plan involves every adult carrying a pistol at all times while inside the compound. When outside of the compound for any reason, our plan dictates that every adult will carry a pistol *and* a rifle. Each adult is responsible for providing his or her own weapons. While inside the camp, each adult stores their rifle in their individual sleeping quarters. We initially considered the idea of storing all rifles in a central "armory" at all times when not in use. But upon further discussion, it made more sense for all men and women to have immediate access to their weapons in the event of a security emergency during the night. While we still do have a room referred to as "the armory", it is used as a secure place to store additional firearms, ammunition, and parts.

In addition to weapons that are intended strictly for security purposes, consider what will be more useful for hunting animals. A good old range rifle is better for hunting larger game than your average AR-15. A shotgun will work better for hunting waterfowl than just about anything else. A bow or crossbow is very handy for hunting when you don't want to make a lot of noise.

Prepper Community

Lastly, I'm sure I don't need to mention cutlery... but I will anyway. If you're anything like me, you've accumulated more pocket knives, sheath knives, and kitchen knives than you can count. Considering this, I'll just say one thing about it: If you don't have at least one quality pocket knife and one quality meat-processing knife, get one!

Chapter 15
New Members After SHTF

Even though you're off the grid, off the beaten path, and off the radar, there's still a possibility that you will encounter other people. There are hundreds of millions of people crawling around this country, and it's truly quite improbable that you can avoid every one of them indefinitely. So what happens if you come across a stranger, or a stranger comes across you? We always talk about the threats posed by desperate or bad people. But what if you come across people who are just like you? What happens when you meet other peaceful people just trying to survive in a troubled world?

The mindset of many dedicated preppers regarding this topic tends to be, "If I don't already know you, I don't want to know you." I think this is a wise mindset to have when survival of you and your group is Priority #1. But I don't dismiss the possibility that you could stumble across a person who may be an asset to your group. I also don't dismiss the possibility that our humanity could trump our OPSEC and compel us to want to save someone's life by bringing them in. Here are a couple scenarios where I could see myself considering someone for membership after SHTF.

Scenario 1: The Homesteaders

Let's say you're out on a run, maybe tracking a nice deer or just exploring the areas outlying your compound. In the distance you see a bit of smoke rising from a chimney. Upon closer investigation, you observe a small farmhouse in the middle of nowhere. Moving closer, and watching through binoculars, you see an old man chopping wood. On the side of his barn hangs trapping equipment. Near the house, a woman who is probably the man's wife comes out and begins washing laundry in an old wash-tub.

These people aren't bothering anybody, and have likely been living a nearly off-grid lifestyle for years. The wealth of skill and know-how in both of their minds is priceless. On the other hand, their age is going to become a major hurdle in their lifestyle if it's just the two of them all alone out here. How many more years of chopping wood does he have left in him? And with no rule of law, it's only a matter of time before somebody stronger comes along and takes from them - probably by force. This seems like a very intriguing scenario in which a partnership could be mutually beneficial.

You may be able to form a rapport with these folks, and eventually convince them to relocate to your retreat. In exchange for security and community, they would provide valuable knowledge and experience in the ways of homesteading. These are not roving, desperate cut-throats. These are skilled gardeners, trappers, hunters, and woodsmen. If trust can be developed on both sides, it would be a match made in heaven!

Scenario 2: The Damsel in Distress

One of your members on security detail reports hearing something that sounds like a baby crying in the distance. Not being made of stone, you assemble a patrol to investigate. A way down the road you come across a young woman trying to comfort a young child. Both of them are visibly ragged and starving. A survey of the area doesn't reveal any clues that this is some sort of ambush or deception. It's simply a starving mother and her starving child. She tells you that she drove until the car ran out of gas, and she's been walking for miles. You really only have two options: Help them, or get comfortable with the fact that they are going to die soon. Even the most hardened of survivalists would have a severe struggle of conscience leaving a helpless child and his mother to die of starvation and exposure. Maybe some water and food is all they need to regain their strength and continue on their way towards wherever they were heading. Or maybe they have nothing, nobody, and nowhere. I think most of us would be forced to think to ourselves, "What's the point is sustaining a small slice of humanity if we aren't capable of being humane?" Whether or not you planned for it, and whether or not she is a valuable asset to the community, you're probably going to be inclined to help them.

These scenarios may be unlikely, but they are possible. Expect the unexpected. People you encounter may be a threat, but they may not be. They may be assets, or they may just be starving and helpless. Whatever the case may be, you have to consider the possibility that you may bring "outsiders" into your community after SHTF. And since it's a possibility, a plan should be in place.

My group's Operational Plan has a section for this very sort of thing. If the day comes where an outsider is brought in, there is an immediate activation of certain protocol. For instance, the newcomers may not be armed initially. Before entering the compound, they must surrender any weapons, and agree to a search of their person and gear. Once inside, they may not leave the compound for a predetermined amount of time. They may not have access to weapons or systems that could be used to harm the group. This initial time will be considered a "probationary period" for the newcomers. During this period, newcomers will be given work details. This serves two purposes, as it gives the newcomers a chance to prove themselves as productive members of the community, and it gives the group a chance to assess their skills and determine how much of an asset (or liability) they will likely be. It will last a minimum of a couple weeks, and will continue until the community agrees that they are an asset and not a liability. During this probationary period, they will be watched closely by members of the group. If they are truly committed to being a part of the community, they will accept this as temporary and necessary for the safety of everyone. Before being accepted as a permanent member, they must have gained the trust of everybody in the community, and every voting member in the community must vote to accept them. Your plan and protocol may differ, but the point is that you must have a plan.

Another issue your group must discuss and come to an agreement on is how to handle things if a person wants to come into your community but you do *not* trust him or her. This is a very serious situation, and it's entirely plausible. Realistically, this scenario is more likely than a scenario where you *do* trust him or her.

You may choose to provide some food, water, or even temporary shelter to a person whom you do not want in your community. Or you may choose to outright deny them assistance of any type. Either way, you don't know how they will react when you inform them that they are not welcome. Even when people are not desperate or hopeless, they have a tendency to take rejection very personally and may react in a very unfavorable manner. Now you have a weary, desperate person who may attempt to access or sabotage your retreat.

If you cast them away, they might head on down the road to find something else. But that's a big gamble for a person who *knows* there are resources just beyond the perimeter to your camp. At the least, you may have a pest on your hands. At worst, you have a dangerous threat to your resources and the safety of your group. So what are you going to do in a situation like this? How will your group handle this potential threat? There is no one answer, and it will surely be a somewhat fluid situation. But it needs to be discussed, and a contingency must be in place so that everybody in the group is in alignment on how it should be handled.

Chapter 16
Disaster Prevention and Recovery

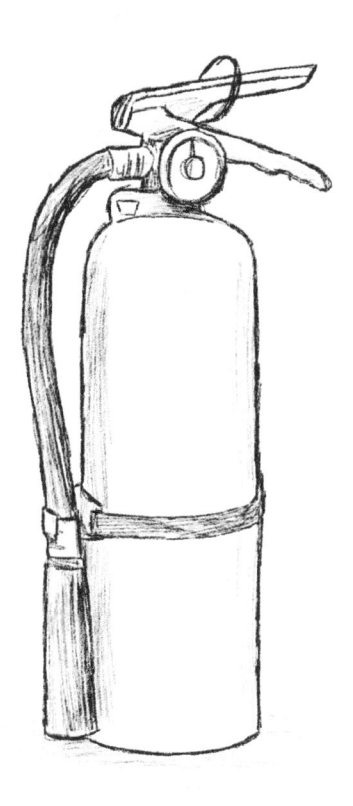

This chapter is all about making sure a hard situation doesn't become harder. Just as we do right now in our normal lives, we must think about how to minimize the potential damages caused by disaster. Call them disasters, acts of God, or whatever you like. Things like weather, accidents, and freak occurrences are a threat to your group's safety and resources.

What are some types of possible disasters that could befall your retreat?

Fire

As long as people have been living indoors, they've worried about fires. House fires are much less common in modern times, because we have much safer heating appliances and electric lighting. But when you rely on burning wood in a stove for heat, and candles and lanterns for light, the risk goes way up. Fire prevention is something that needs constant vigilance. Basic common sense must be employed because your lives and resources are on the line. Things like water buckets or fire extinguishers should be in every structure. Burning stoves should never be left unattended. Additionally, your group should have a plan that details how a blaze will be handled. Will you employ a bucket brigade? If you have running water, do you have hoses easily accessible? Lastly, what will you do if an entire structure burns down? If it's your only structure, you are now quite literally out in the cold.

Storms and Flooding

High winds and storms can cause incredible damage to homes and other structures. Heavy rains can cause flash floods very quickly. You need a plan for what to do if you lose shingles, windows, or any other building material to storms. If water begins flooding in to your living area, how will it be handled? You can't call your insurance company, and there are no disaster recovery crews on the way.

Pests

Likely to be mainly a risk to areas in which you have food or garbage, pests are a real concern. In the old days, mice and rats were a severe problem. They carry disease and spread germs. Insects will also cause a very bad day if they manage to infiltrate your food supplies. Generally speaking, you can mitigate your risk of pest problems by keeping all food items securely sealed and stored, and getting rid of your garbage before it can attract any unwanted guests. Except when being prepared or eaten, seal all food in rigid containers. As soon as you create garbage, burn it or bury it. Just don't let it pile up within your camp!

Structural Failure

While less likely than fires and mice, it's not beyond the realm of imagination that a serious structural failure of some sort could happen. This could be a rotting beam that supports your cabin's roof. It could be the foundation settling beneath an outbuilding. If you are faced with a dangerous structural hazard in one of your buildings, it will need to be addressed. For the sake of your group's safety and valuable resource at risk of collapsing, quick measures will be needed to repair the problem. Repairing such things without heavy equipment and elaborate materials may be difficult or impossible. If it can't be fixed or patched-up, will you be able to abandon that structure entirely?

Chapter 17
Morale

I think it's not unfair to say that modern-day people take many things for granted. It's nobody's "fault". It's pretty much to be expected, considering the world we live in. Each of us is a product of the times, so to speak. We don't have to spend even a second thinking about if we will eat today. We don't have to worry about not having heat, light, toilets, or entertainment. These things are darn-near guaranteed in our society. Every waking minute of the day, we are bombarded with opportunities to eat, drink, socialize, and occupy our minds. Social media, smart phones, and video games make it so our minds are never idle. We can't sit still and quiet for 2 minutes without pulling out the phone and fiddling away. Also, most modern Americans do not have a physically-laborious day-to-day life.

If SHTF, we suddenly jump into a forgotten era of hard work and few conveniences. It will be a shock to our systems, physically and emotionally. It won't take too long before members of your group begin to wonder, "What's the point of it all?" That is to say, some people will struggle greatly with their situation. They may wonder if a life absent of modern luxuries is a life worth living. That is why paying attention to morale is so important.

If people aren't happy at least some of the time, it leads to a toxic environment. A toxic environment leads to the downfall of your group's survival. This place you've created is meant to be a sanctuary, not a labor camp. You've brought people together to form a community, and at the end of the day that's how everyone should feel.

As a group, you should come up with some ideas of how you will work on keeping up morale. Every group will have different ideas about what will improve their emotional wellbeing. It will also be a fluid thing, and it will be difficult to prepare for changing moods and feelings. Here are a couple of things that my group has discussed with regards to working on morale after the retreat has been activated:

Recreation

There's no question that a homesteading lifestyle during a troubled period of societal collapse will require a lot of work, all the time. Every single day will involve labor, worry, and otherwise dealing with the very serious situation at hand. For the emotional stability of your community's inhabitants, you have to make it a point to engage in some lighthearted activities as time permits. Particularly for the younger members of your group, having a little fun and fostering positivity will go an incredibly long way in maintaining morale. It doesn't take long for us humans to start thinking, "If there's no such thing as fun or enjoyment, what's the point?" The point is survival, but we have to keep our minds active and healthy in order to keep our perspective on why.

Consider what recreational activities you can enjoy within your camp. Board games, decks of cards, and music can occupy lots of downtime indoors. Things like Frisbees, soccer balls, and other sporting equipment are great for a bit of outdoor fun. Discuss it with your group. It's even a great opportunity to get the kids involved in retreat prepping. Simply pose the question, "What fun activities do you like to do that don't need electricity?" They'll hopefully spit out a long list of ideas.

Hobbies for the adults are important as well. Maybe stamp collecting is off the table, but there are plenty of opportunities to take up more rustic hobbies. Whittling, bird watching, and writing are some activities I'd embrace having more time in which to partake. Whatever you come up with, it's important to keep your mind stimulated. If you get into a daily grind of trudging water buckets and chopping firewood after being accustomed to a lifetime of modern conveniences, morale will take a hit quicker than you'd think.

Uniforms

Who doesn't like to feel that they are a part of something? Our group decided to implement some semblance of a "uniform" because it makes people feel a bit special. We feel that it strengthens our bond as a group. While some might argue that it's unproductive to foster an "Us vs. Them" attitude, a survival situation sort of requires it to some extent.

I mentioned in a previous chapter that everybody in the group wears some type of woodland camouflage. There is no requirement on which specific camo each person wears, as long as it is some type of woodland pattern. I don't, however, consider this to be the uniform of our community. The uniform takes the form of an embroidered patch that each member can sew onto his or her own jacket. Each member gets a couple patches. Not only does it help our people feel more like a unified group, but it adds a bit of theatrics to the whole thing. I tend to be of the opinion that a certain degree of theatrics and fanfare help make a situation feel a little less somber. Uniforms, flags, group names, and rallying cries are all potential ways for the individuals in your group to feel tied together as one. This whole thing works because of community, so don't neglect the little things that will make your group feel like one.

Chapter 18
Recommended Resources

As I've said throughout this book, my aim is to get your wheels turning and your juices flowing. There's no realistic way for one book to cover every intricacy of all possible aspects to bugging out, living off-grid, and surviving in a post-SHTF homestead. Throughout every chapter, I have presented many things you must consider if you want to go all the way in your prepping efforts. If it's something that you truly want to work towards, then your journey has just begun. From here, you owe it to yourself to gain as much additional knowledge as possible. Aside from first-hand experience and mentorship, the most valuable resources I've found to learn about the many different aspects of prepping and homesteading are books, websites, and internet videos. There is a limitless ocean of knowledge out there, and you just have to go grab it!

While not a comprehensive list by any means, I wanted to share a few of the resources that I've found particularly useful, interesting, and/or unique.

David Kobler

Perhaps known best by his YouTube handle, "SouthernPrepper1", David Kobler is an army veteran, survivalist, homesteader, author, and preparedness consultant. His YouTube channel has over 500 videos and over 20 million views. While he is not shy about discussing politics, David Kobler is a field-tested expert in most things "prepping," and he shares his knowledge and perspective about long-term survival in any way he can.

In addition to his YouTube channel, David Kobler has written two books: *Retreat Security and Small Unit Tactics* and *The Seven Step Survival Plan*. Both are available on Amazon.

The Total Outdoorsman

For decades, Field & Stream has published various editions of a book titled *The Total Outdoorsman*. While it touches on dozens of various aspects of hunting, fishing, camping, and survival, it's a decent resource for learning about a lot of different things. Especially helpful for people who have not spent a lot of time in the wilderness, these books have tons of tips and essential knowledge to remain warm, dry, fed, and alive.

From my observations, most people have absolutely no experience with processing an animal. Unless you're a hunter and have processed game, you're not going to have a clue what to do with an animal after killing it. Whether or not you reference a *The Total Outdoorsman* book, you owe it to yourself to become familiar with the basics of dressing and butchering some of the most common game animals.

PrepperGroups.com

In addition to being an informational forum and resource for prepping in general, the www.preppergroups.com website is a fantastic meeting place for precisely the type of like-minded people who are also looking to start or join a prepping community. You can browse by state and read posts from preppers near you, or you can create your own post.

While other social media platforms have various groups and pages for every topic of interest (including prepping), this website is geared 100% to the sort of people who are interested in a survival community.

Reddit.com

Reddit is a community of over 200 million unique users. The website is part content aggregator and part social media. Within the Reddit community, there are over a million sub-communities (known as subreddits) that range in every conceivable topic, hobby, interest, and geographical location. Dozens of these communities are dedicated to prepping, homesteading, survival, and everything in between. These communities are comprised of dedicated users who are passionate about prepping. The open discussions and knowledge sharing are an invaluable resource, particularly for people who are newer to prepping.

In addition, there are individual prepping-specific communities that are narrowed down even further to geographic locations. At the time of this writing, there are 14 region-specific prepping subreddits for the United States alone.

ARRL

The American Radio Relay League is a non-profit organization comprised of amateur radio enthusiasts. If you want to learn about ham radio, this is the place to start. Radio communications are an incredible resource to have in an emergency situation, and getting your amateur radio license is the perfect way to learn.

ARRL is a membership association, but you can take advantage of most resources on their website for free. Check it out at www.arrl.org.

NRA

Whether you want to contribute to the preservation of our Second Amendment rights, or you want to learn about firearms training and safety, the NRA is unquestionably the place to go. Founded in 1871, the NRA is the largest firearm training and competency organization in the United States. Boasting over 5 million members, the NRA is also among the oldest civil rights organizations, fighting to ensure Constitutionally-guaranteed freedoms for law-abiding Americans.

To learn about firearm training courses, visit www.firearmtraining.nra.org.
To become a member of the NRA and support American gun ownership, visit www.nra.org.

The Red Cross

First aid training is one of the most valuable skills to have when outside help is unavailable. Find training classes in your area on the Red cross website at www.redcross.org. The Red Cross also provides free disaster response and recovery training for all volunteers. You must contact your local Red Cross office to learn more about their free disaster training.

FEMA

A branch of the United States Department of Homeland Security, FEMA is the Federal Emergency Management Agency. Their primary objective is to respond to disasters in the United States and coordinate recovery efforts. When a natural or man-made disaster has overwhelmed local and state agencies, FEMA steps in to provide support. In the meantime, FEMA provides data and knowledge about emergency preparedness and disaster recovery.

Learn more about FEMA at www.fema.org.
Visit FEMA's civilian disaster preparedness website at www.ready.gov.

Other Books and Information

While I don't have one specific recommended resource for each of these, I recommend learning about the following topics. Depending on your role in the community, you may need to go deep and learn as much as possible. At the very least, it's wise to become somewhat familiar with each of these areas. This is by no means an exhaustive list, but it's a great place to start if you're new to the concept of long-term prepping.

- Gardening - Don't forget about container gardening and growing vegetables in a greenhouse.
- Composting - While necessary for gardening, composting is a beast all its own.
- Food preservation - Canning, dehydrating, and all the other ways to make food keep longer.
- First aid - What to do for basic injuries and illness, and also more severe trauma in the field.
- Herbal medicines and other natural remedies - Goes hand in hand with first aid knowledge.

- Cook books - After processing game and growing veggies, learn a variety of ways to prepare it.
- Bushcraft - Learn knot-tying, and how to make useful things from natural materials.
- Foraging edible plants - Be able to identify fruits, nuts, berries, roots, fungus, and other edible plants in the wild.
- Small animal farming - Chickens, rabbits, goats, etc. Learn what it takes to keep them healthy and happy.
- Organization and logistics - Learn the basics of staying organized so your retreat runs like a well-oiled machine.
- Solar energy and alternative power sources - Understand how to set up an off-grid electrical system.
- Repair manuals - Be prepared to maintain and fix your small engines and other equipment.

Made in the USA
Coppell, TX
05 December 2023